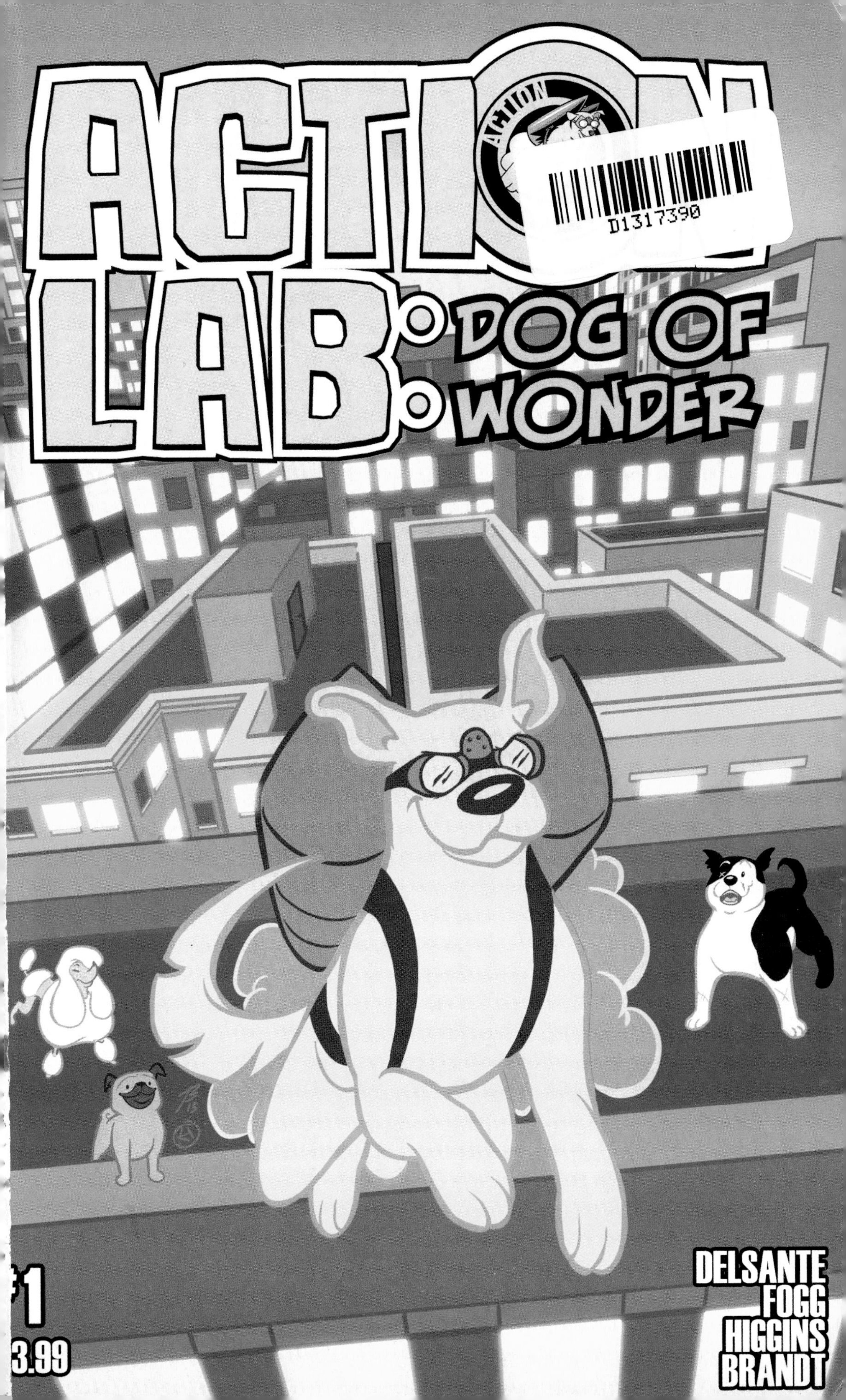
ACTION LAB: DOG OF WONDER
#1
3.99
DELSANTE
FOGG
HIGGINS
BRANDT

FROM ALL-AGES TO MATURE READERS
ACTION LAB HAS YOU COVERED.

 **Appropriate for everyone.**

 **Appropriate for age 9 and up. Absent of profanity or adult content.**

 **Suggested for 12 and Up. Comics with this rating are comparable to a PG-13 movie rating. Recommended for our teen and young adult readers.**

 **Appropriate for older teens. Similar to Teen, but featuring more mature themes and/or more graphic imagery.**

 **Contains extreme violence and some nudity. Basically the Rated-R of comics.**

FIND YOUR NEW FAVORITE COMICS.

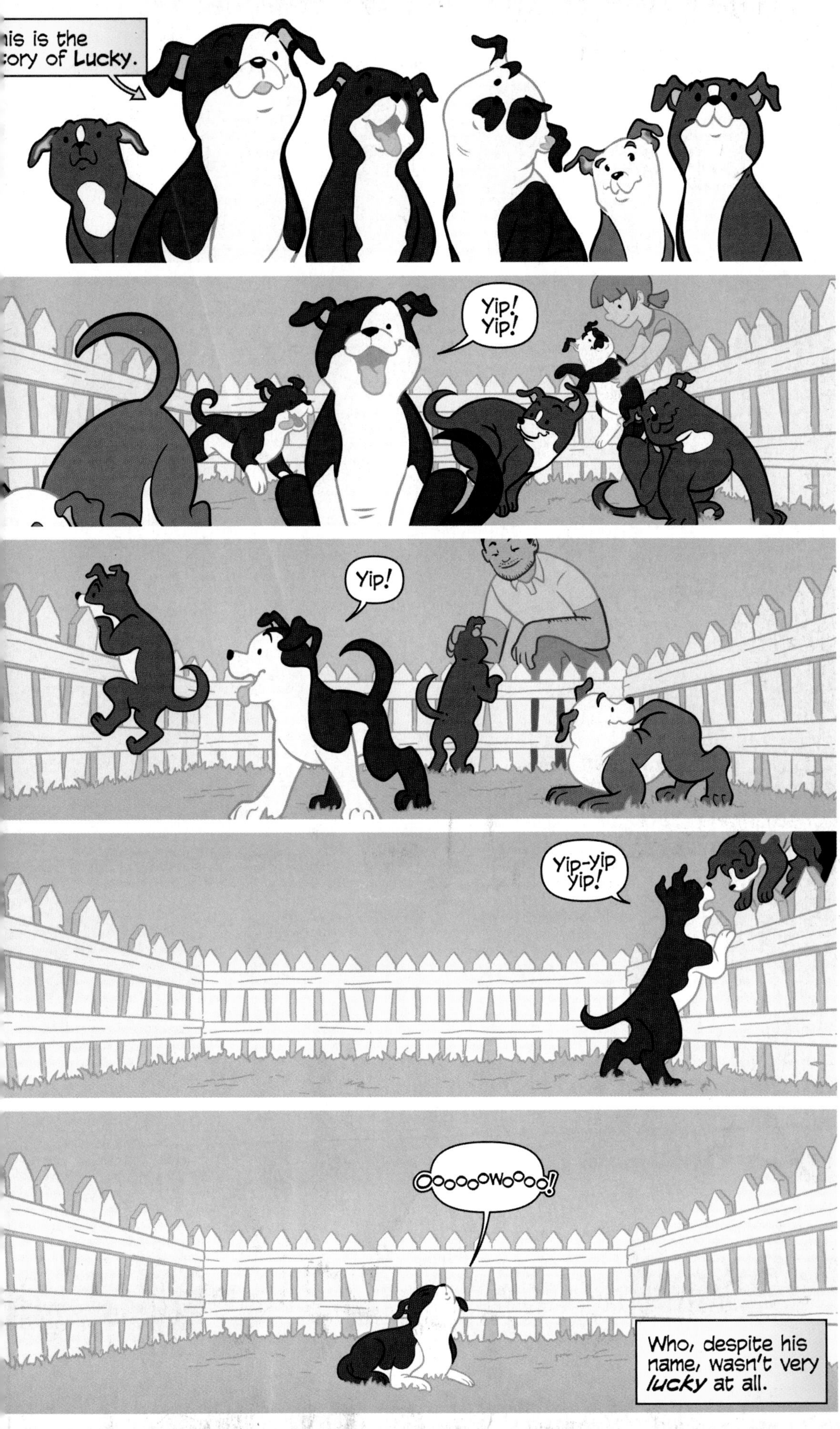

his is the
tory of Lucky.
Yip! Yip!
Yip!
Yip-yip yip!
OooooOWoOoo!
Who, despite his name, wasn't very *lucky* at all.

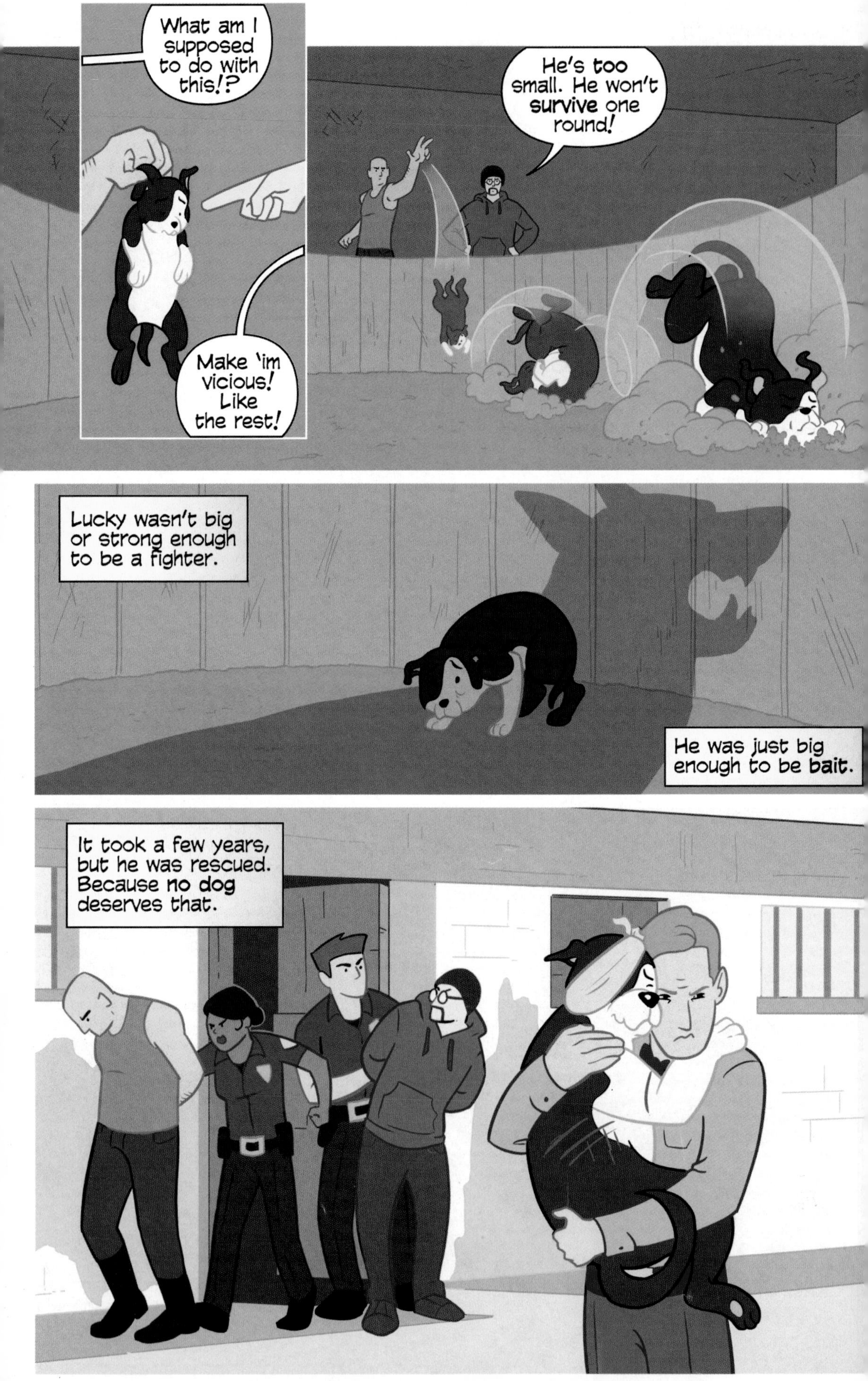
What am I supposed to do with this!?
He's **too** small. He won't **survive** one round!
Make 'im vicious! Like the rest!
Lucky wasn't big or strong enough to be a fighter.
He was just big enough to be **bait.**
It took a few years, but he was rescued. Because **no dog** deserves that.

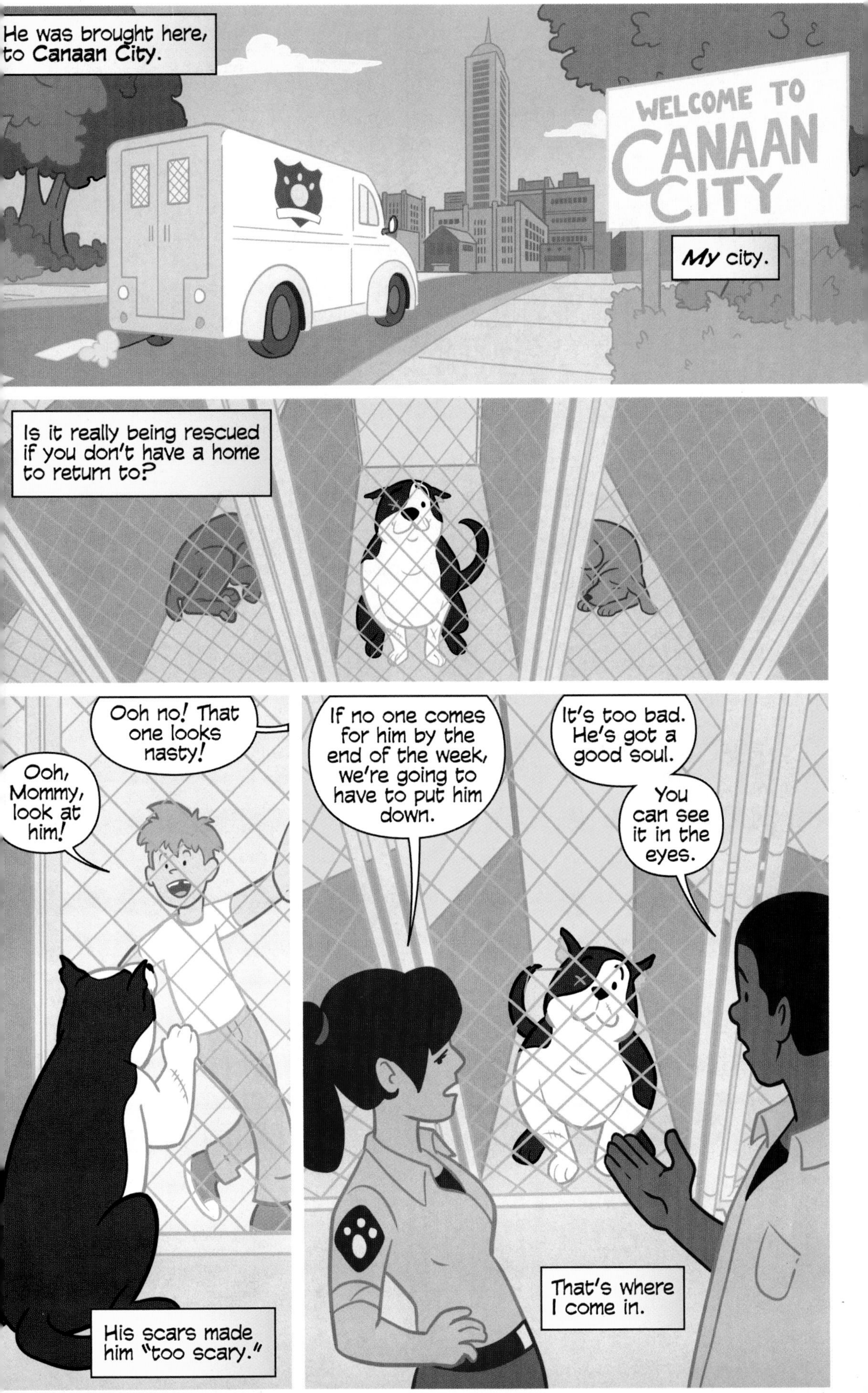

He was brought here, to Canaan City.
WELCOME TO CANAAN CITY
My city.
Is it really being rescued if you don't have a home to return to?
Ooh no! That one looks nasty!
Ooh, Mommy, look at him!
His scars made him "too scary."
If no one comes for him by the end of the week, we're going to have to put him down.
It's too bad. He's got a good soul.
You can see it in the eyes.
That's where I come in.

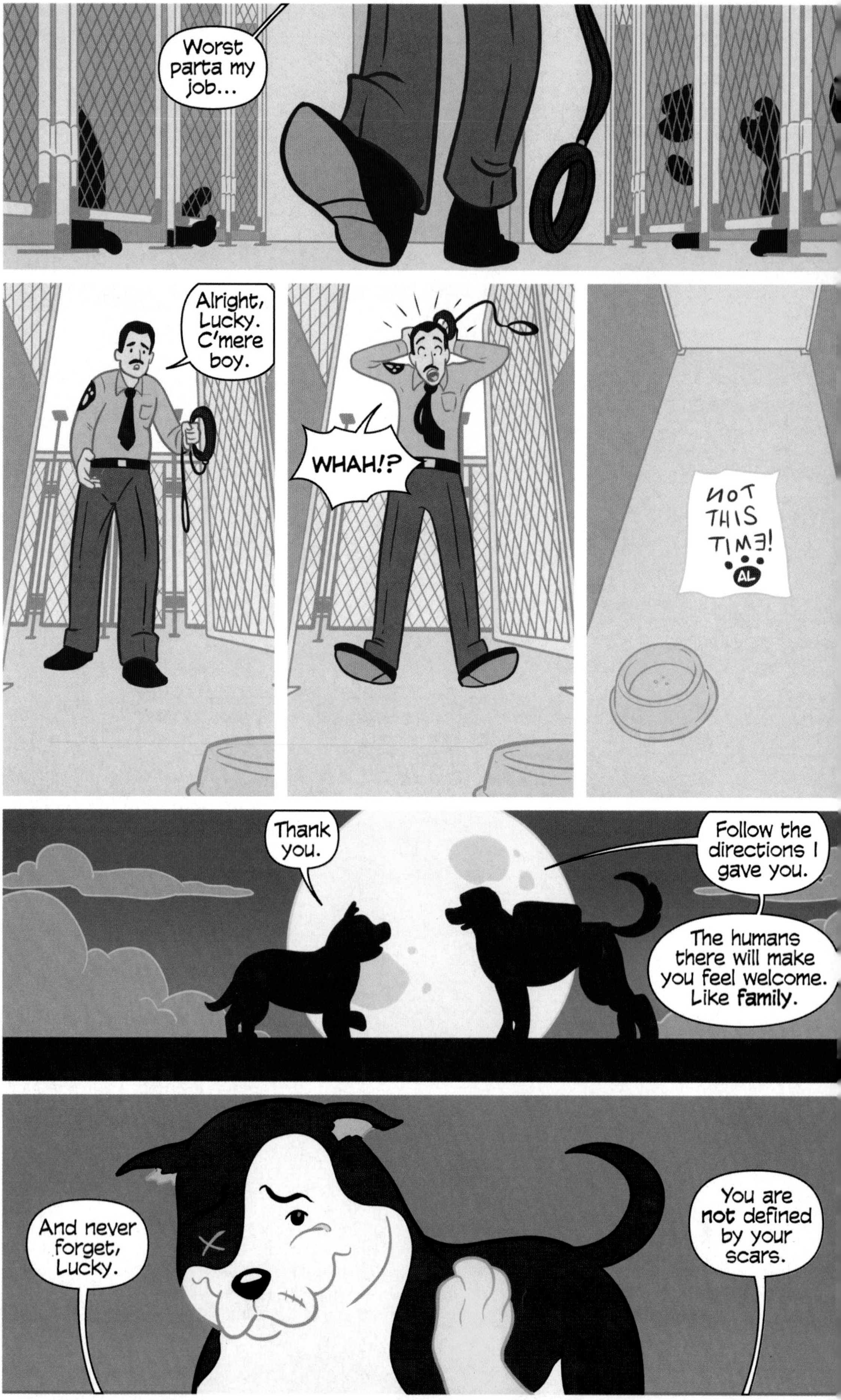

Worst parta my job...
Alright, Lucky. C'mere boy.
WHAH!?
NOT THIS TIME!
AL
Thank you.
Follow the directions I gave you.
The humans there will make you feel welcome. Like **family**.
And never forget, Lucky.
You are **not** defined by your scars.

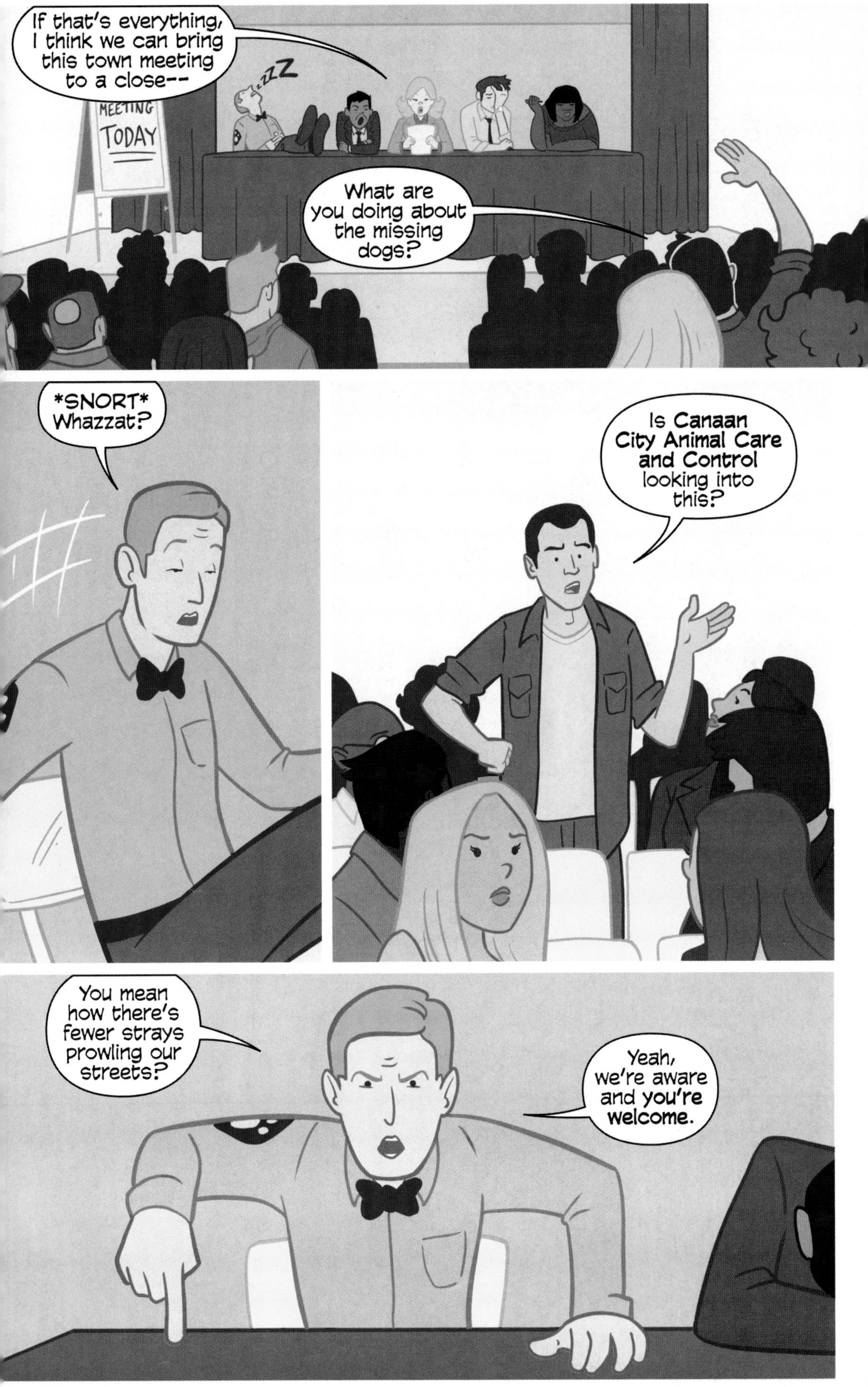

If that's everything, I think we can bring this town meeting to a close--
ZZZ
MEETING TODAY
What are you doing about the missing dogs?
SNORT Whazzat?
Is **Canaan City Animal Care and Control** looking into this?
You mean how there's fewer strays prowling our streets?
Yeah, we're aware and **you're welcome.**

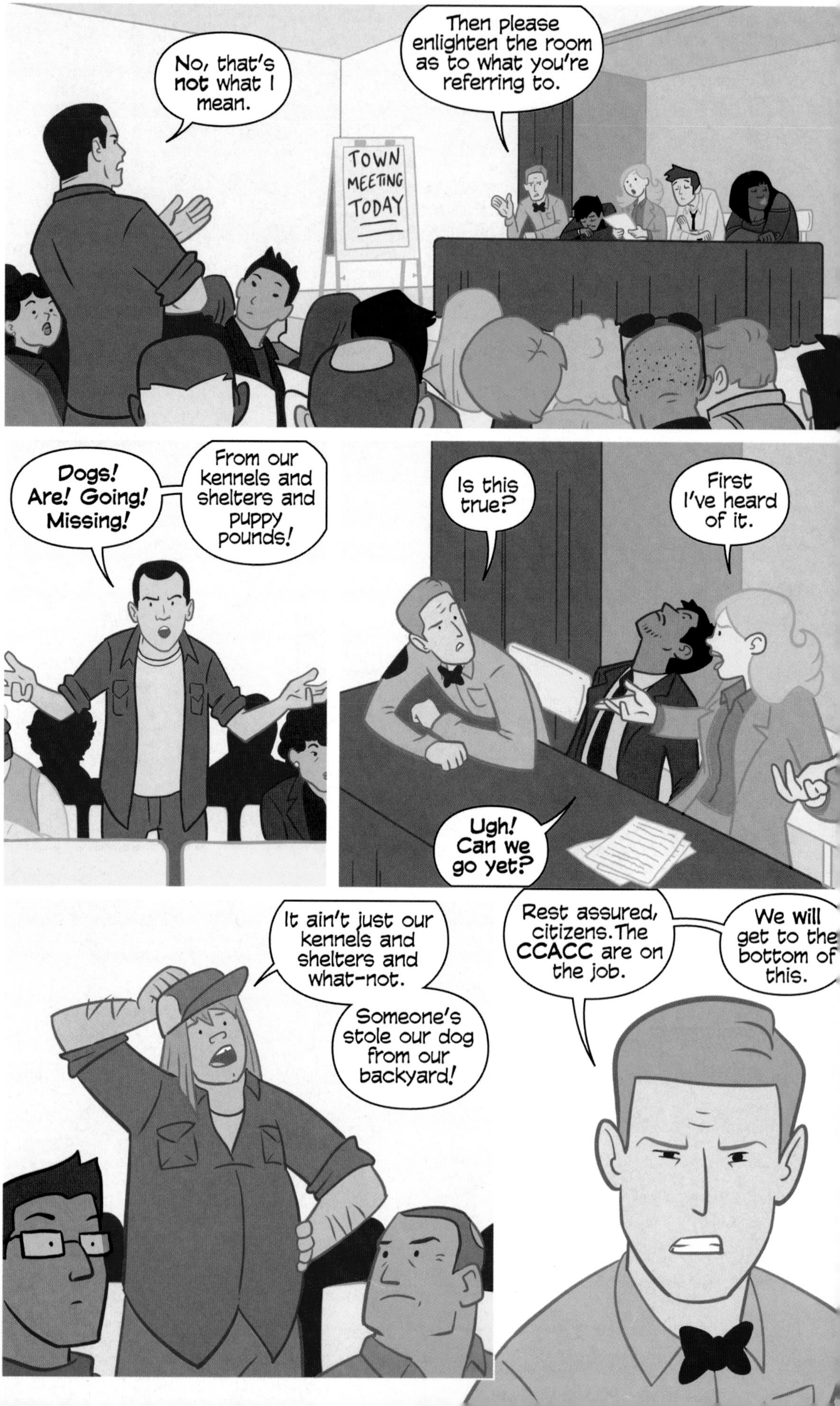
No, that's **not** what I mean.
Then please enlighten the room as to what you're referring to.
TOWN MEETING TODAY
Dogs! Are! Going! Missing!
From our kennels and shelters and puppy pounds!
Is this true?
First I've heard of it.
Ugh! Can we go yet?
It ain't just our kennels and shelters and what-not.
Someone's stole our dog from our backyard!
Rest assured, citizens. The **CCACC** are on the job.
We will get to the bottom of this.

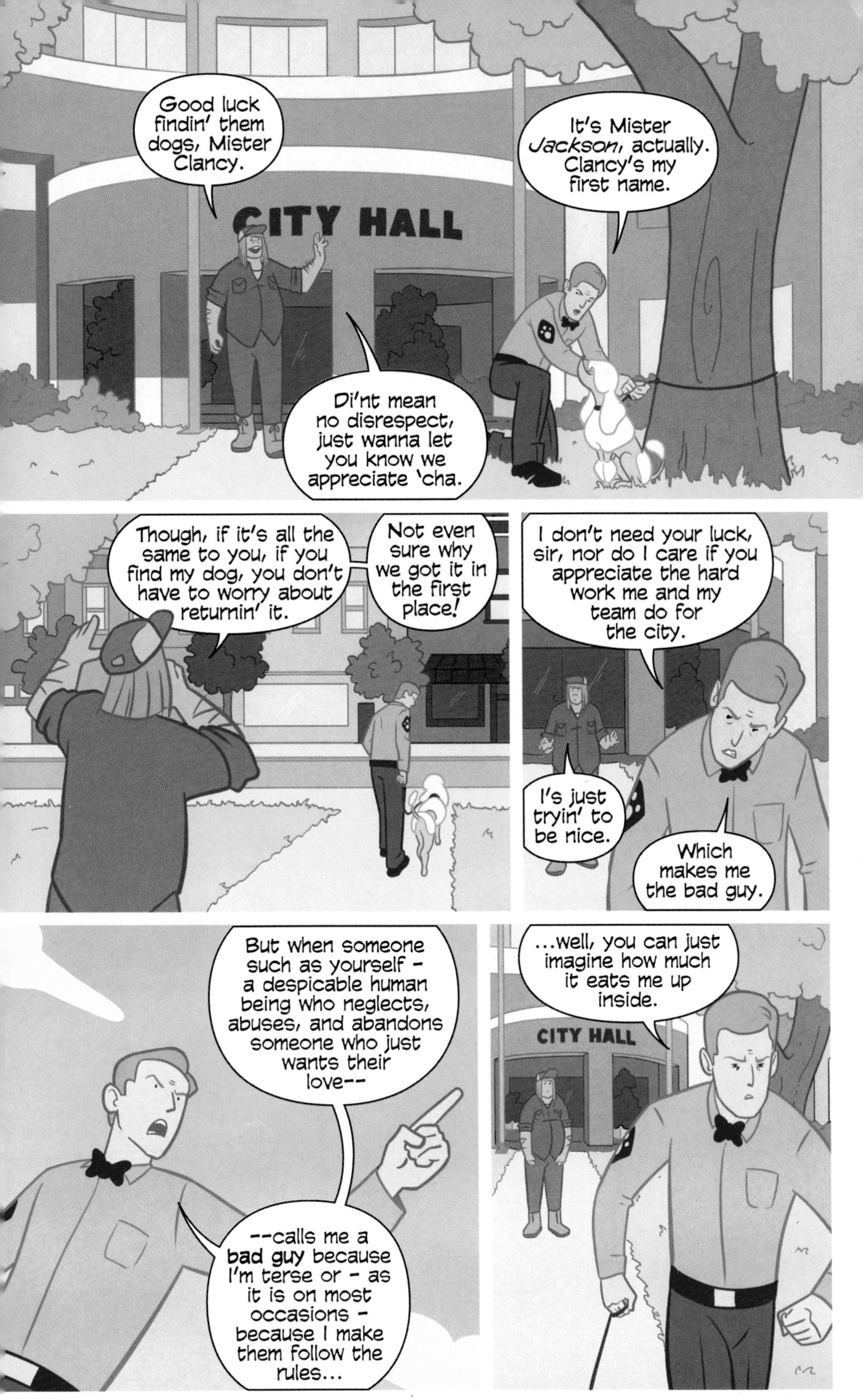
Good luck findin' them dogs, Mister Clancy.
CITY HALL
It's Mister Jackson, actually. Clancy's my first name.
Di'nt mean no disrespect, just wanna let you know we appreciate 'cha.
Though, if it's all the same to you, if you find my dog, you don't have to worry about returnin' it.
Not even sure why we got it in the first place!
I don't need your luck, sir, nor do I care if you appreciate the hard work me and my team do for the city.
I's just tryin' to be nice.
Which makes me the bad guy.
But when someone such as yourself - a despicable human being who neglects, abuses, and abandons someone who just wants their love--
--calls me a bad guy because I'm terse or - as it is on most occasions - because I make them follow the rules...
...well, you can just imagine how much it eats me up inside.
CITY HALL

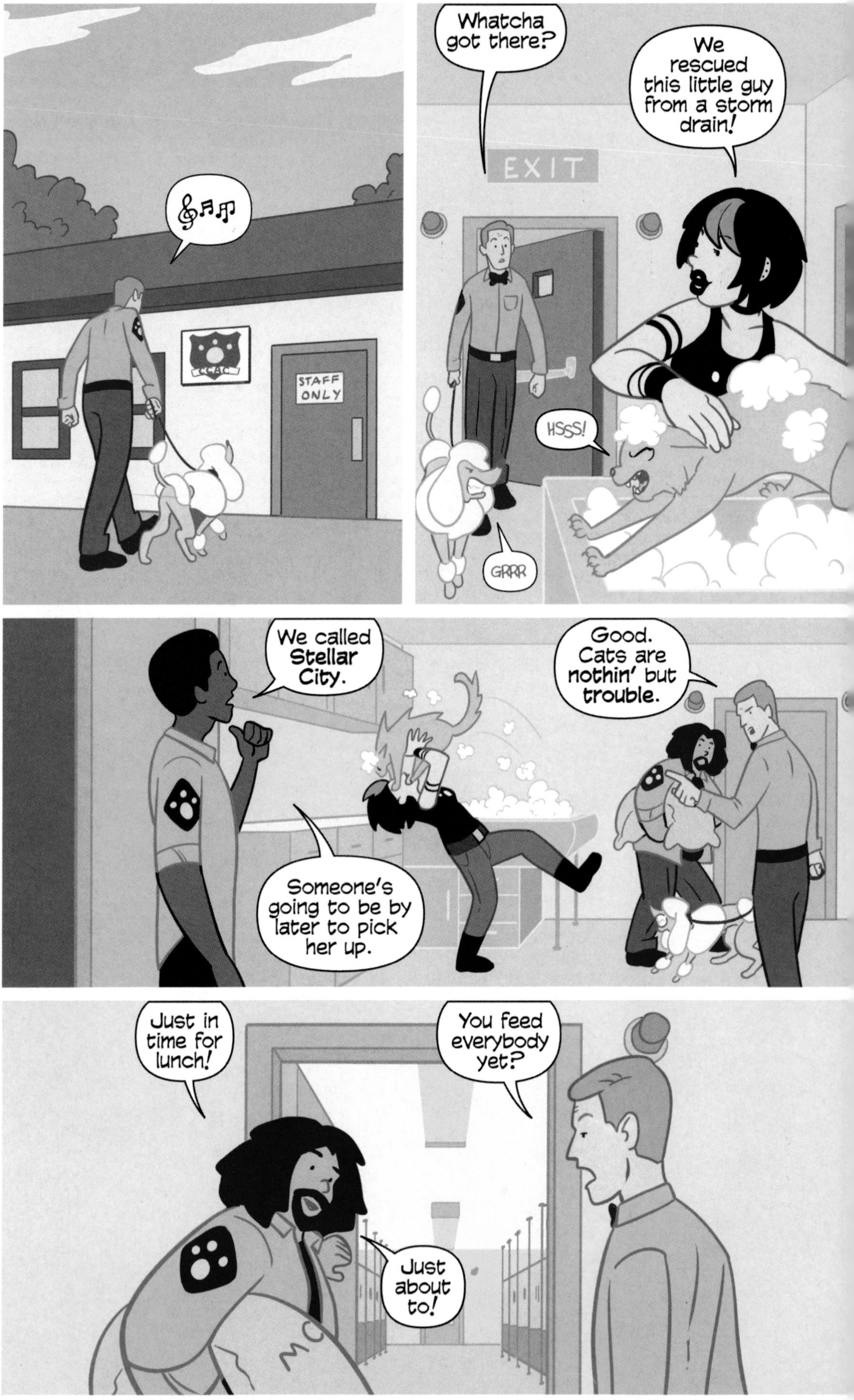
CCAC
STAFF ONLY
Whatcha got there?
EXIT
We rescued this little guy from a storm drain!
HSSS!
GRRR
We called **Stellar City**.
Good. Cats are **nothin'** but **trouble**.
Someone's going to be by later to pick her up.
Just in time for lunch!
You feed everybody yet?
Just about to!

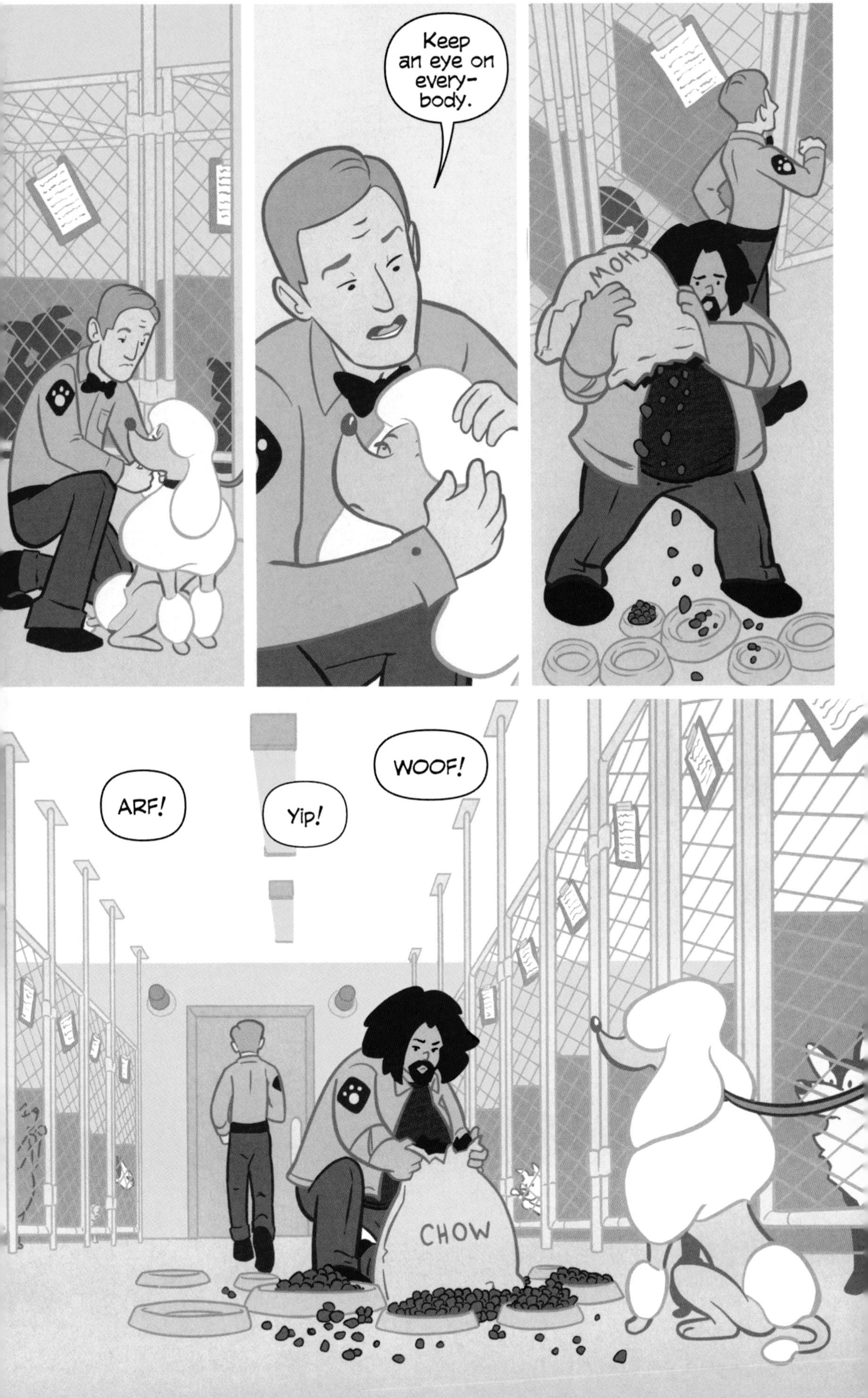
Keep an eye on every-body.
CHOW
ARF!
Yip!
WOOF!
CHOW

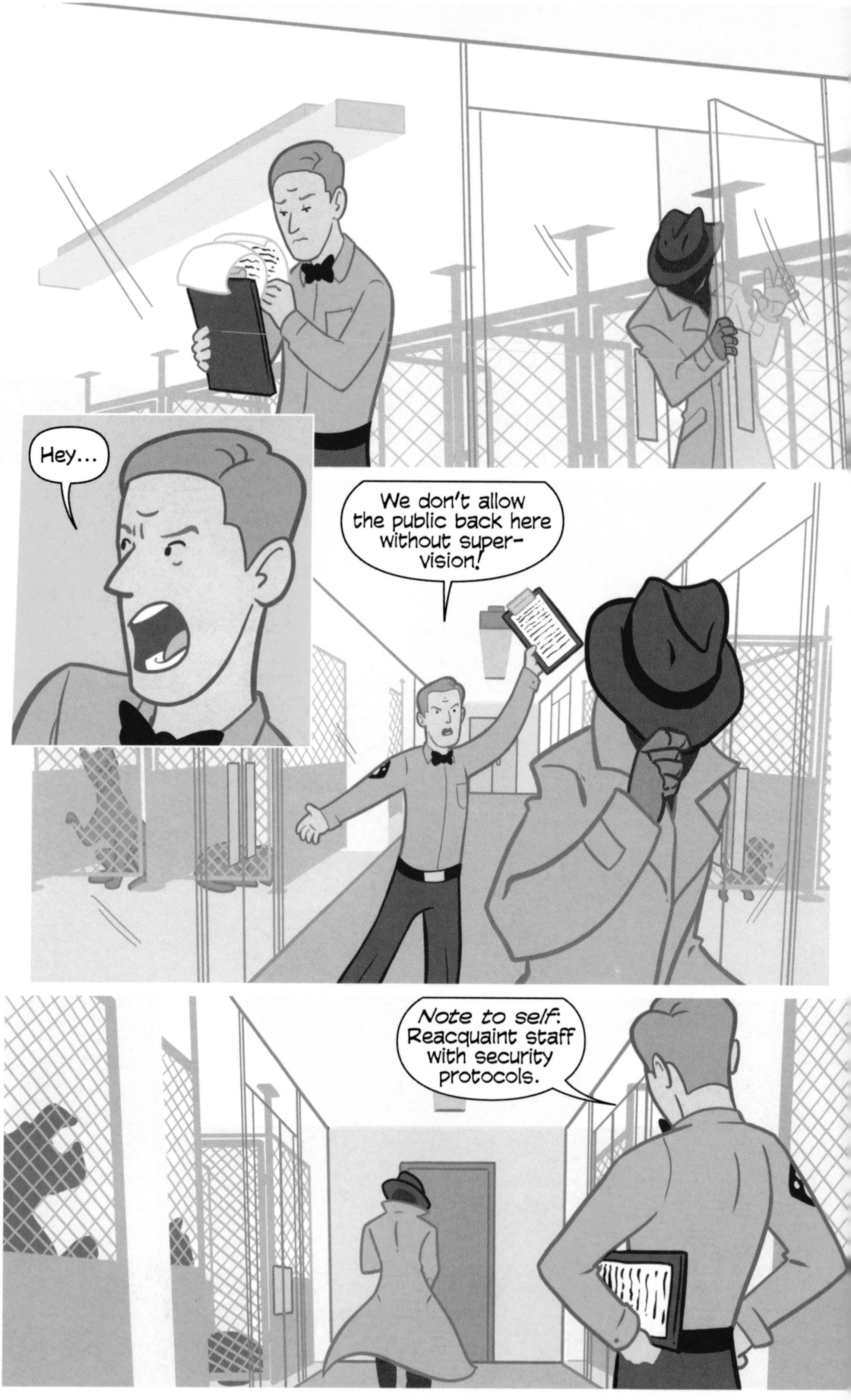
Hey...
We don't allow the public back here without super-vision!
Note to self: Reacquaint staff with security protocols.

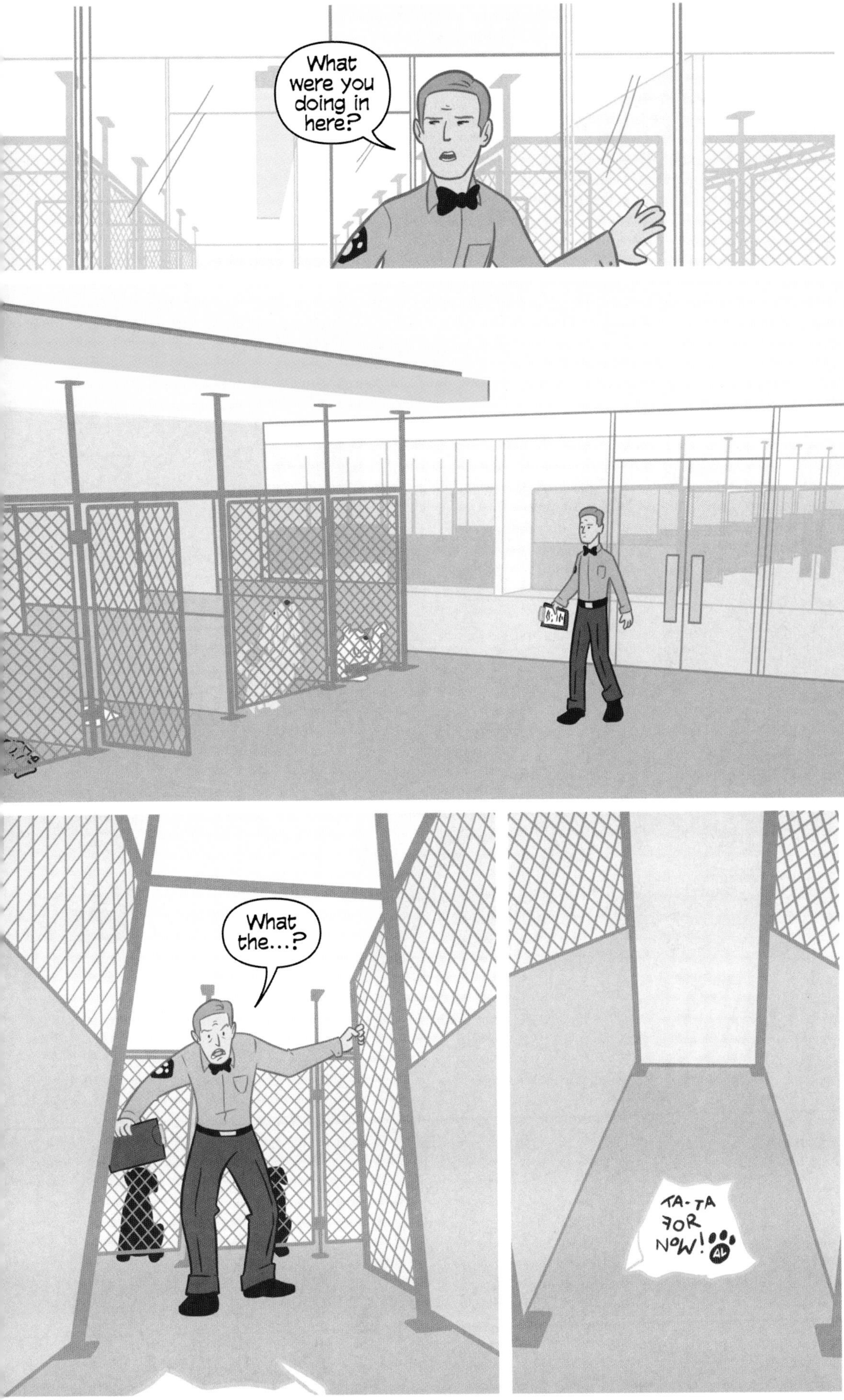
What were you doing in here?
What the...?
TA-TA FOR NOW!
AL

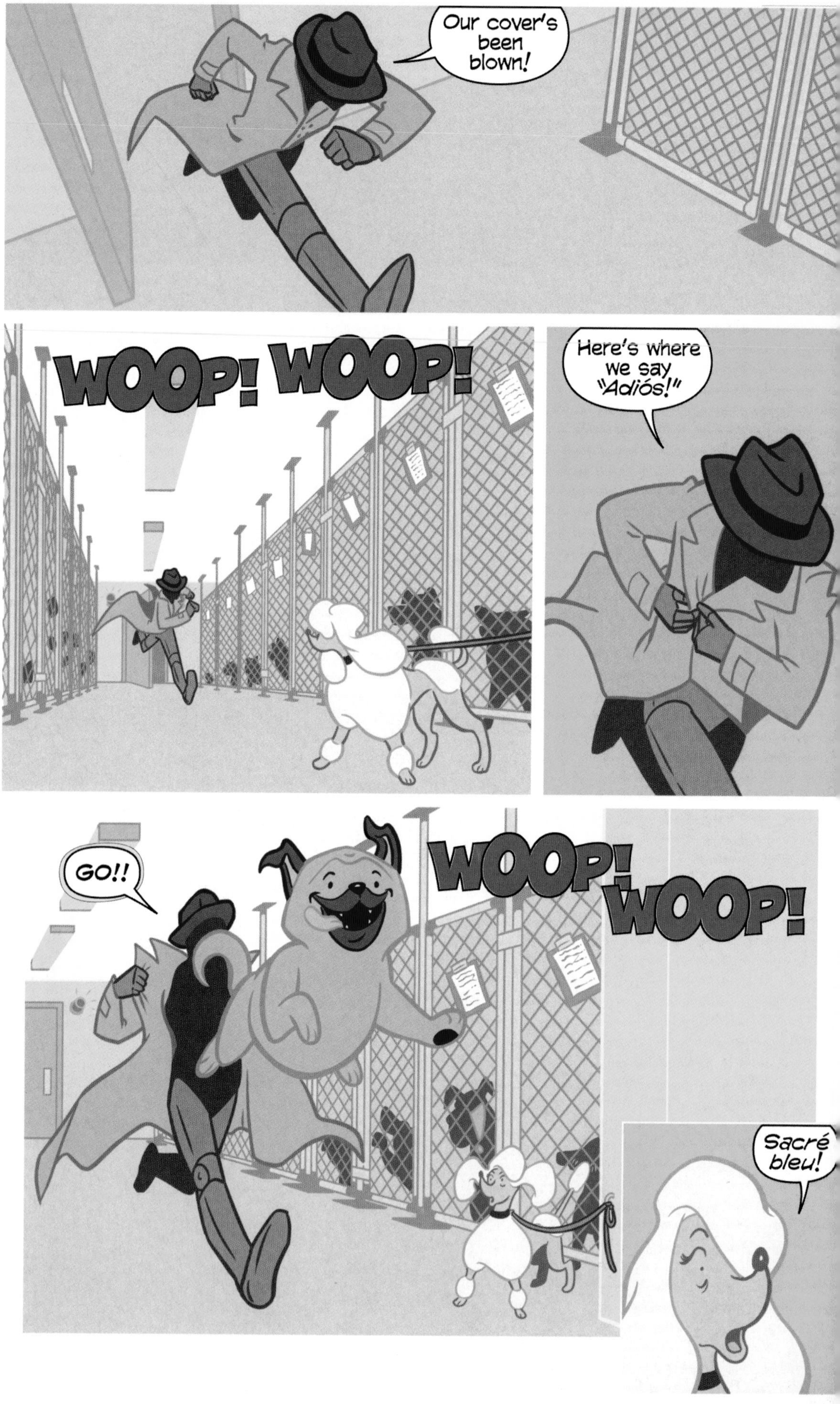

Our cover's been blown!
WOOP! WOOP!
Here's where we say "Adiós!"
GO!!
WOOP! WOOP!
Sacré bleu!

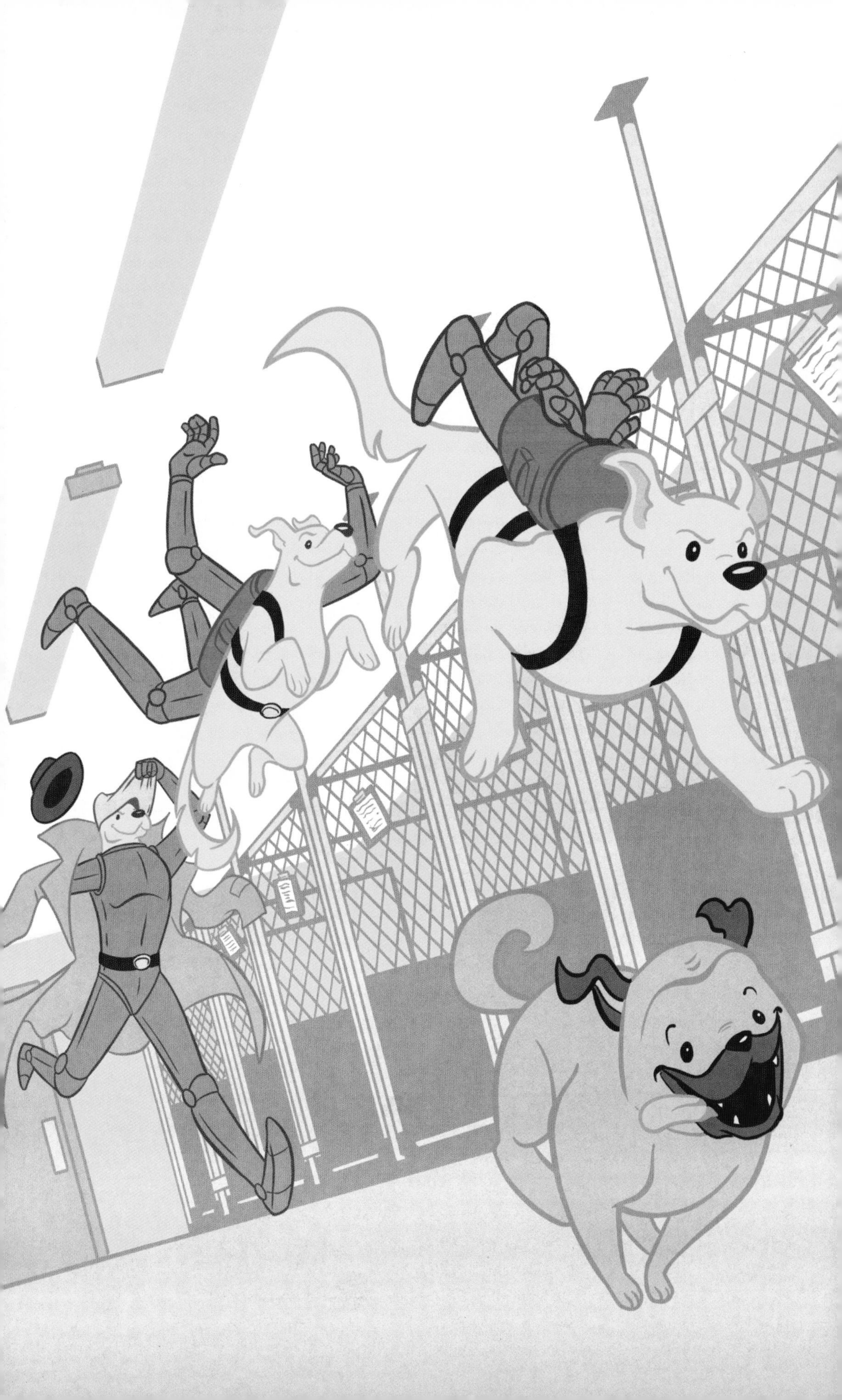

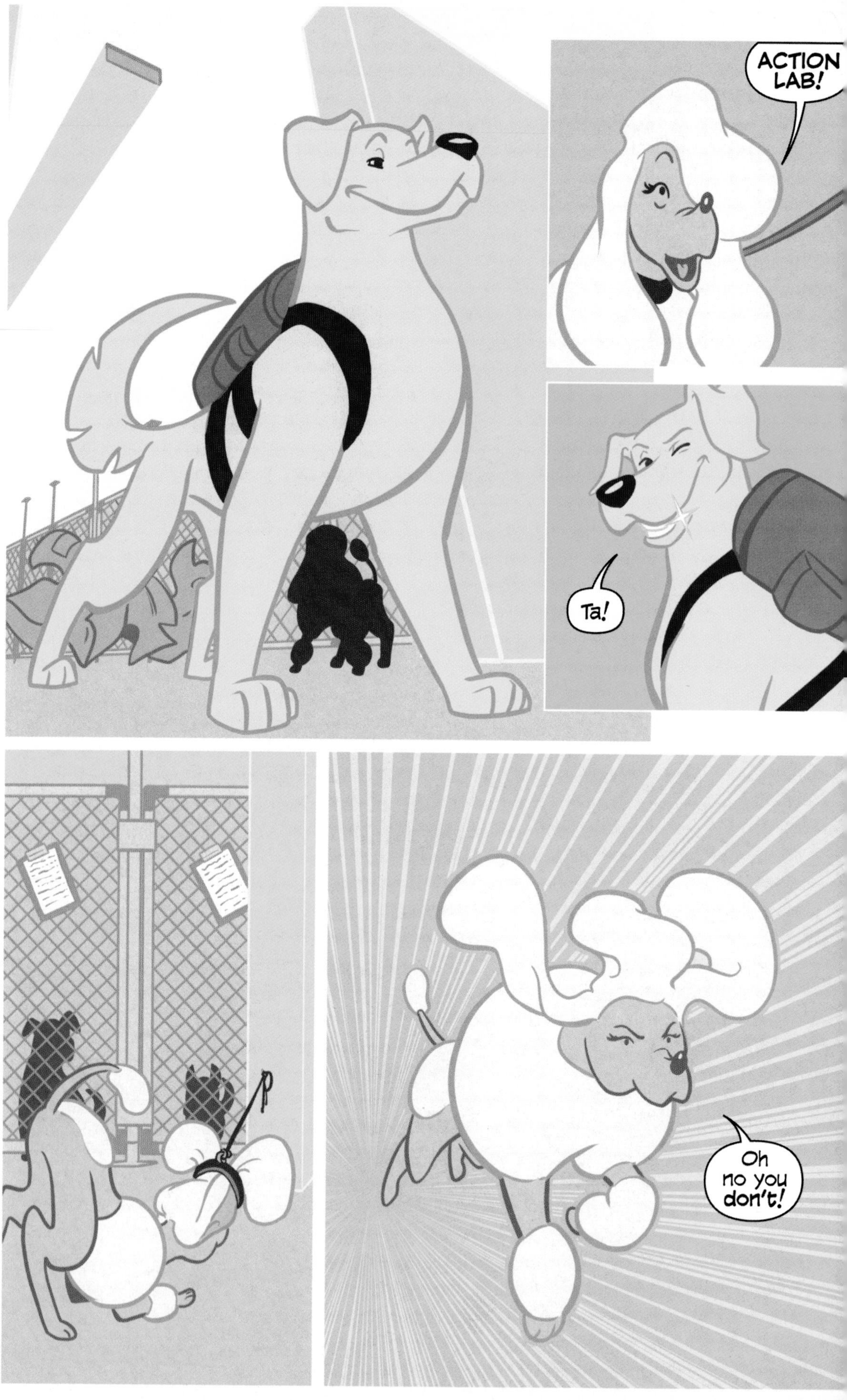
ACTION LAB!
Ta!
Oh no you don't!

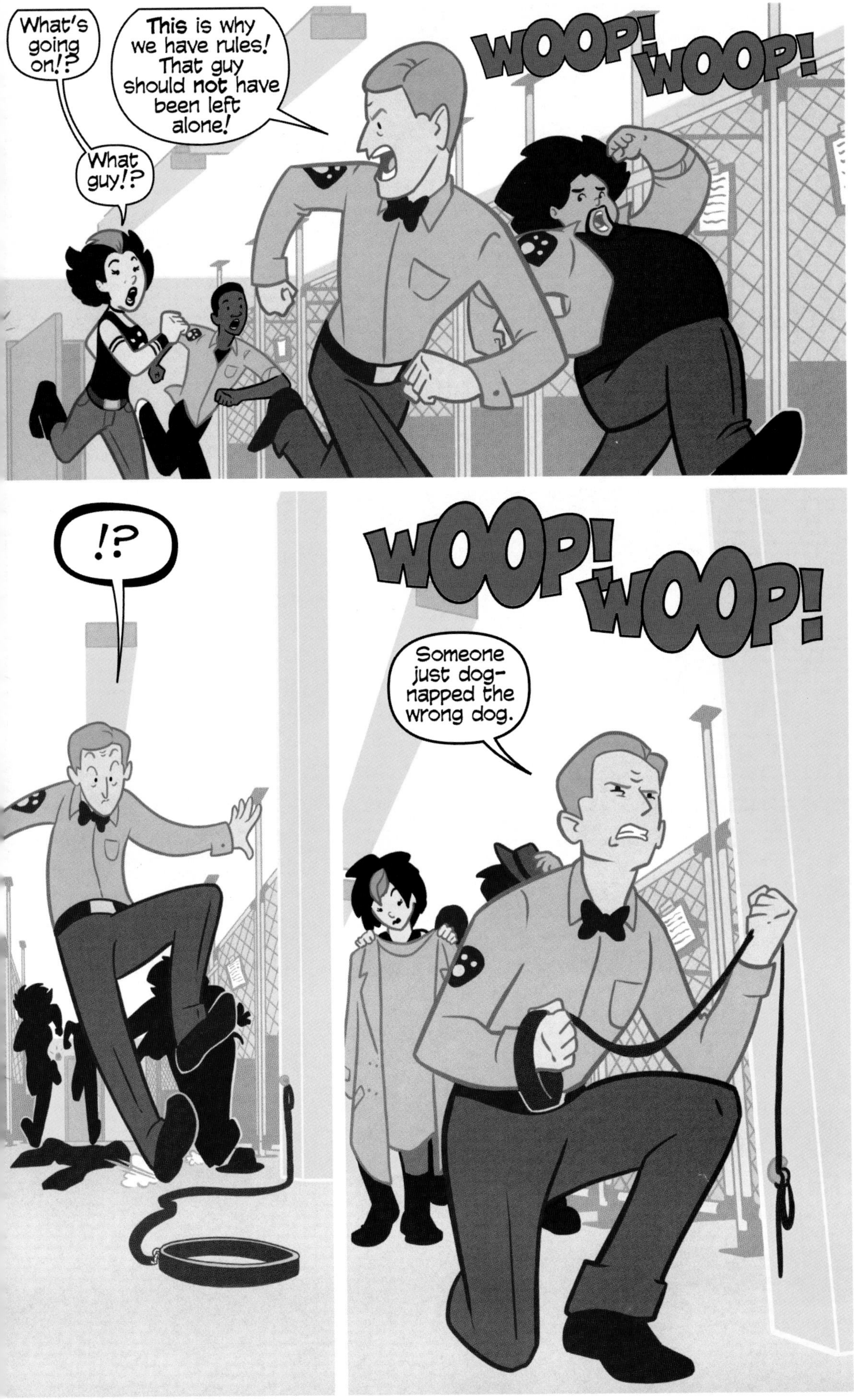
What's going on!?
This is why we have rules! That guy should not have been left alone!
What guy!?
WOOP! WOOP!
!?
WOOP! WOOP!
Someone just dog-napped the wrong dog.

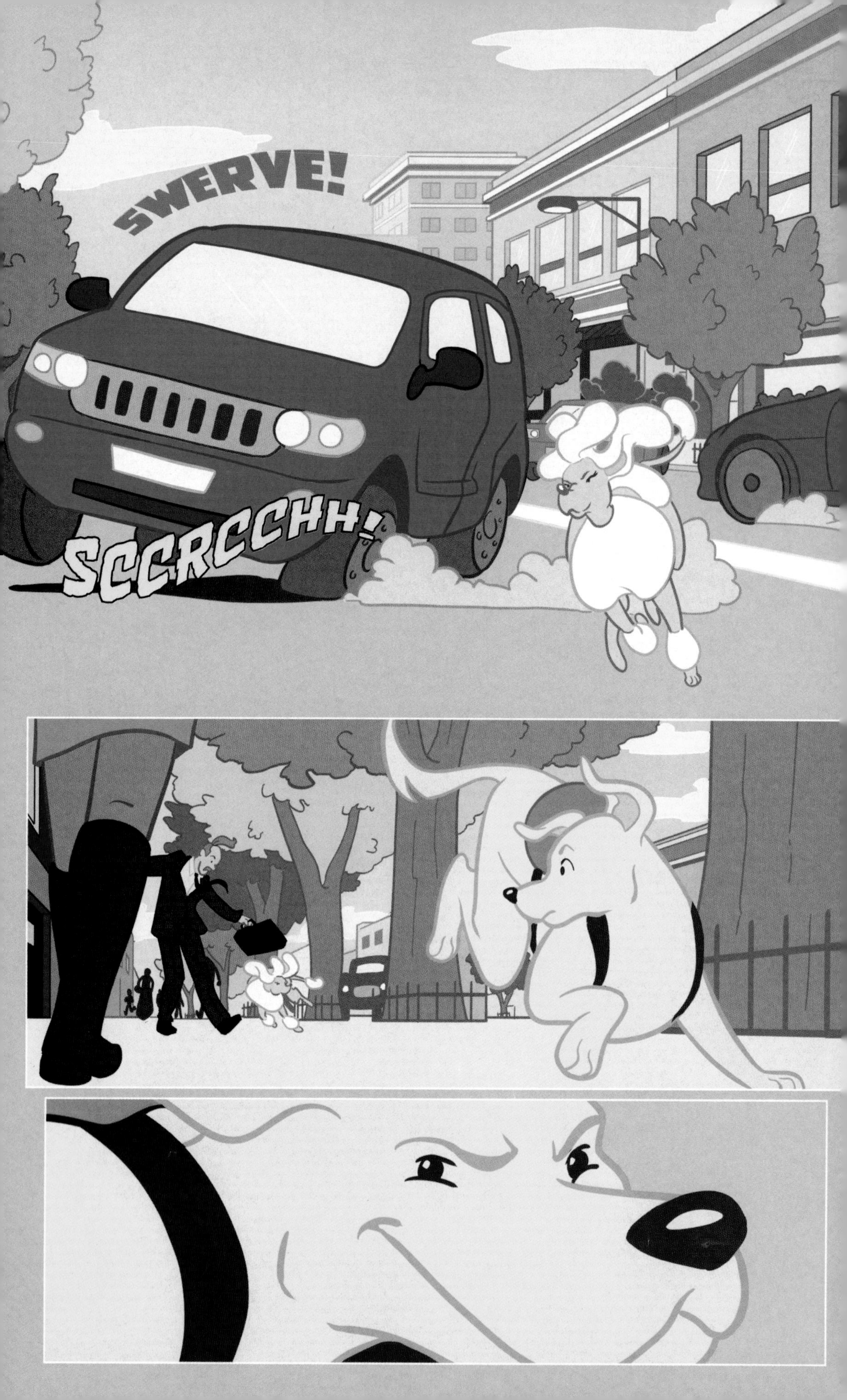
SWERVE!
SCCRCCHH!

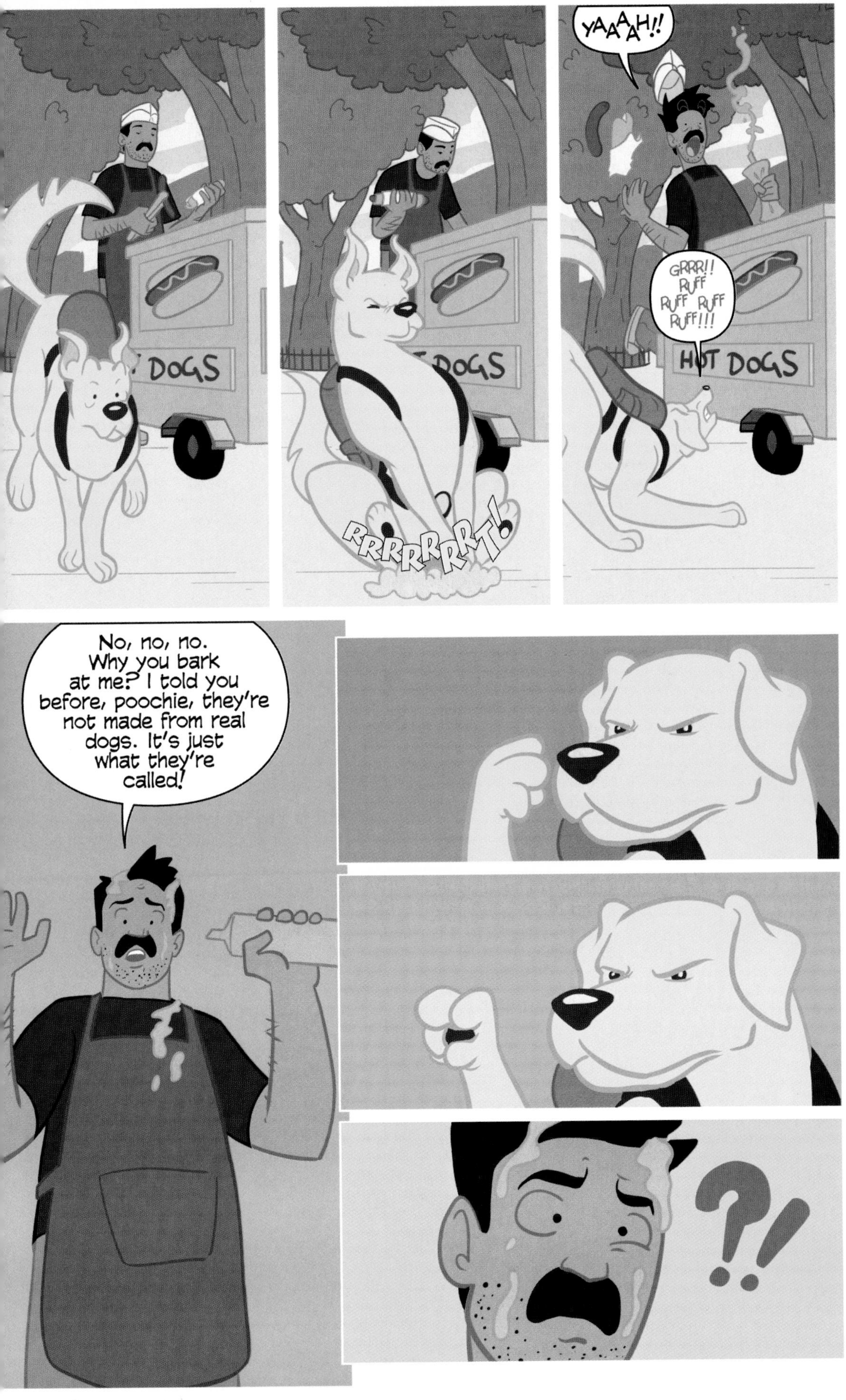

RRRRRRRRT!
YAAAAH!!
GRRR!! RUFF RUFF RUFF RUFF!!!
HOT DOGS
No, no, no. Why you bark at me? I told you before, poochie, they're not made from real dogs. It's just what they're called!
?!

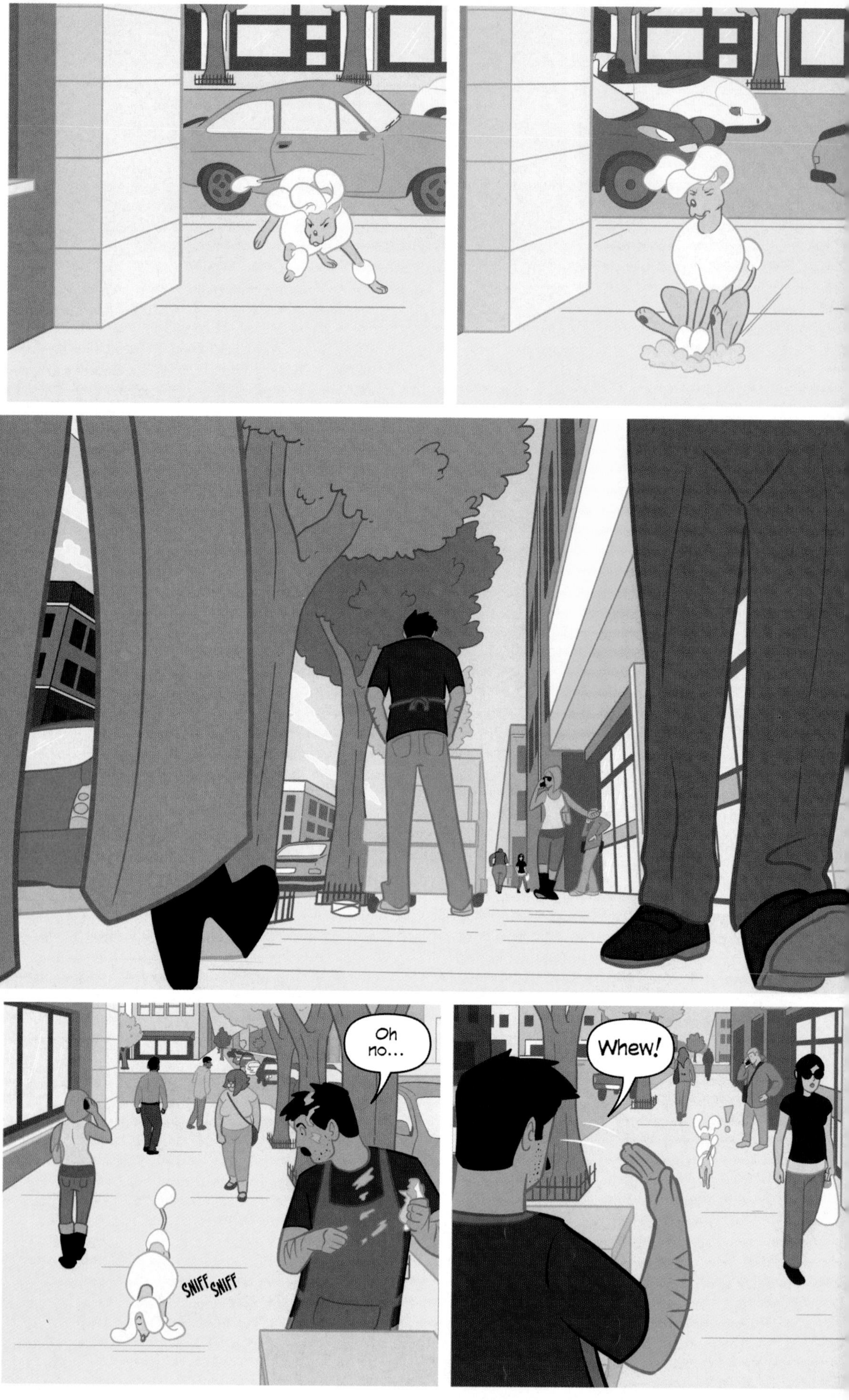
Oh no...
SNIFF SNIFF
Whew!
!

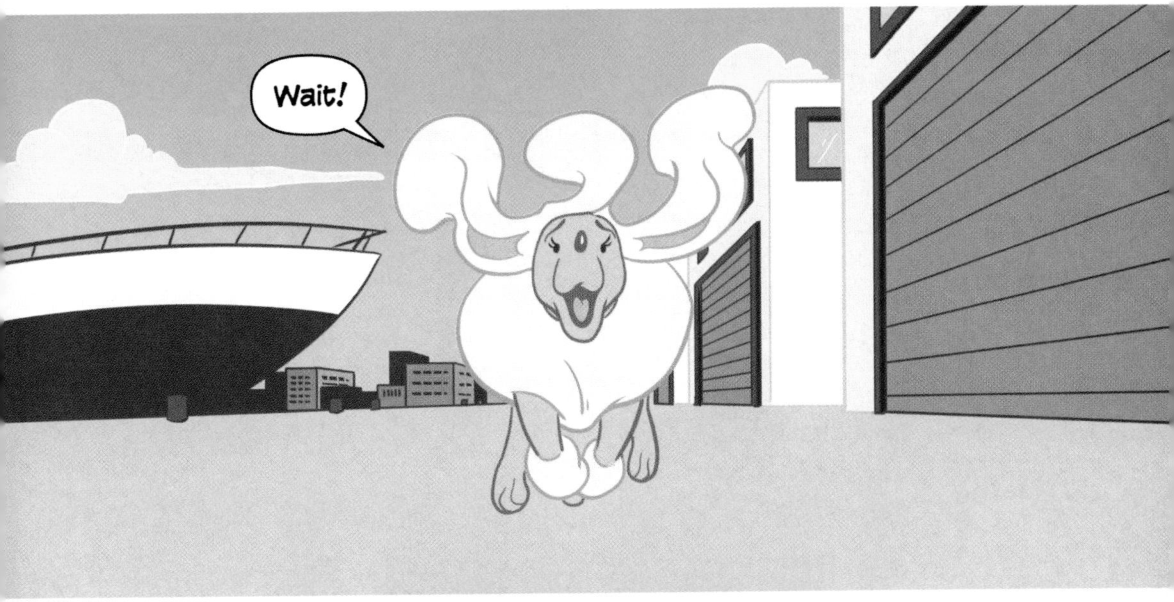
Wait!

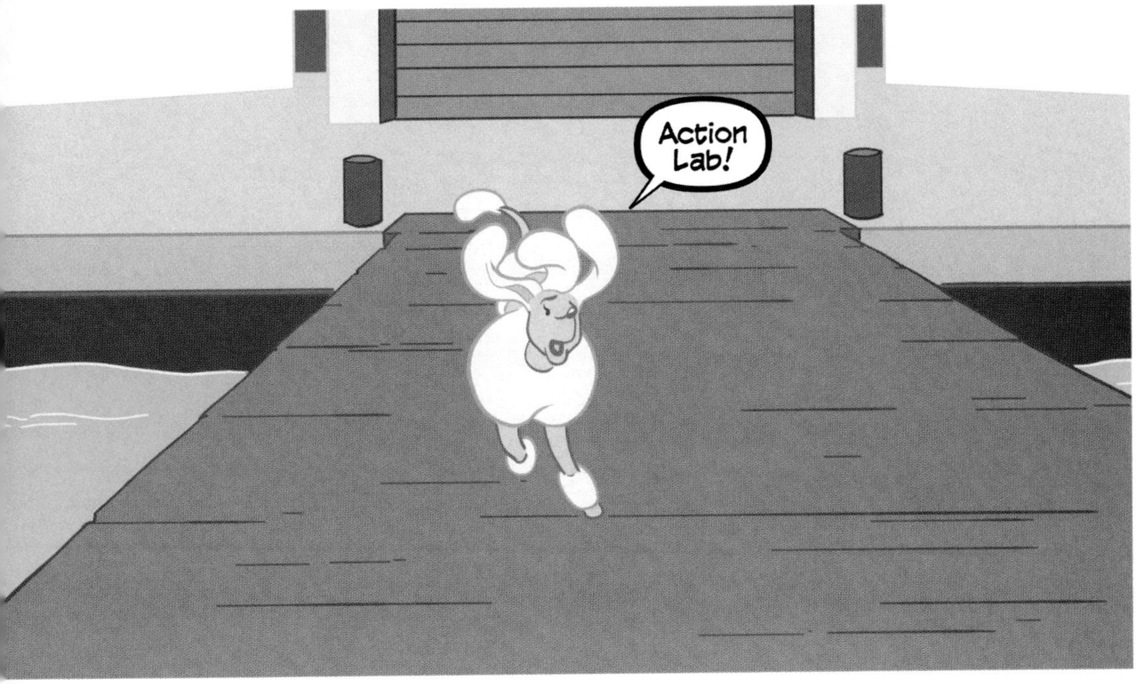
Action Lab!

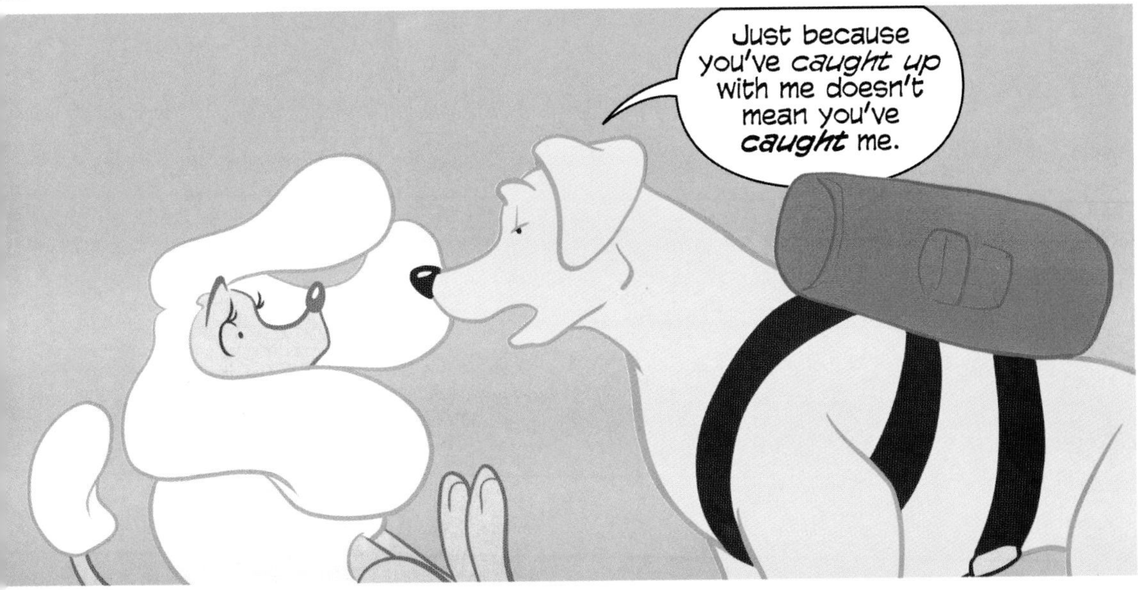
Just because you've *caught up* with me doesn't mean you've ***caught*** me.

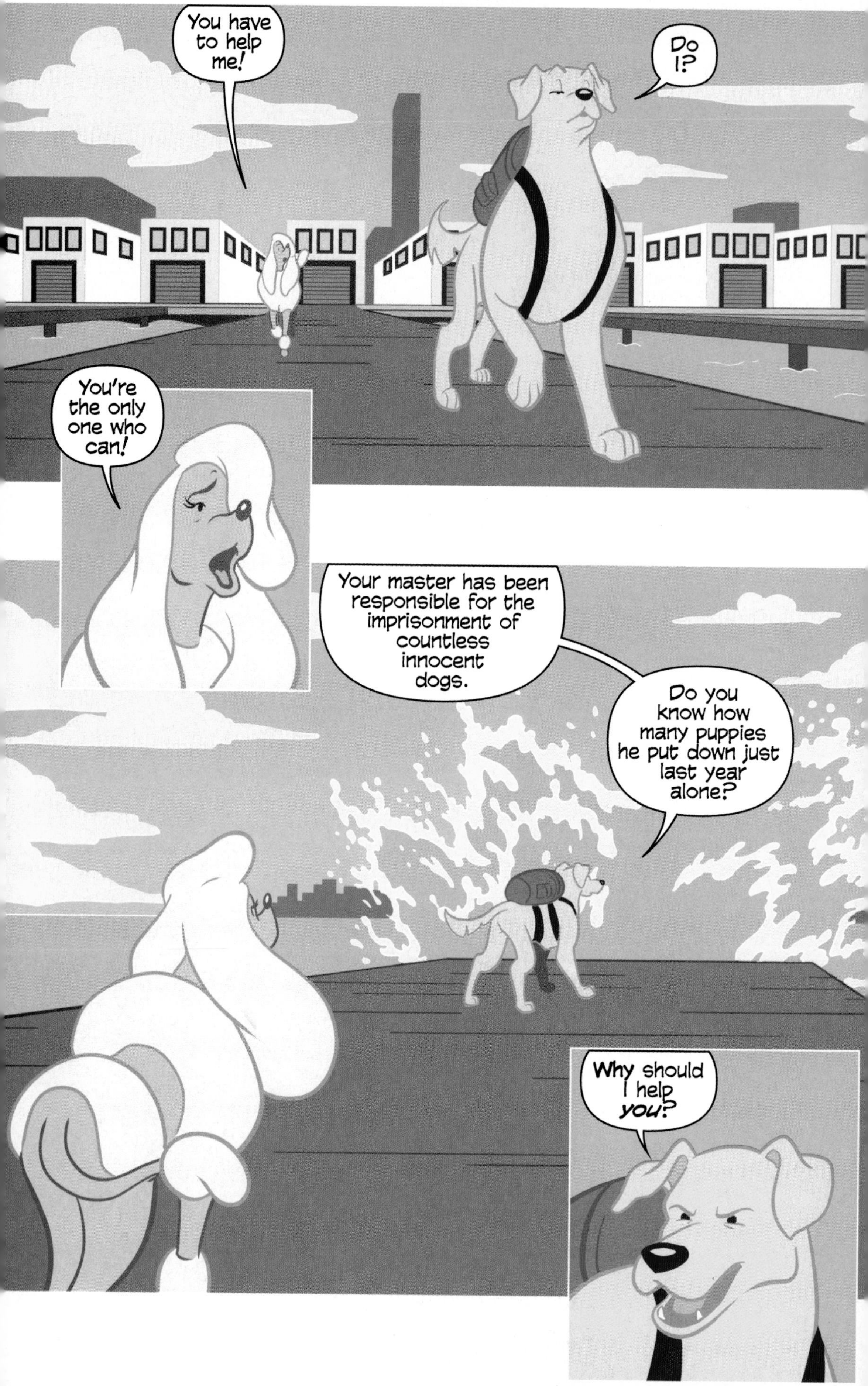
You have to help me!
Do I?
You're the only one who can!
Your master has been responsible for the imprisonment of countless innocent dogs.
Do you know how many puppies he put down just last year alone?
Why should I help *you*?

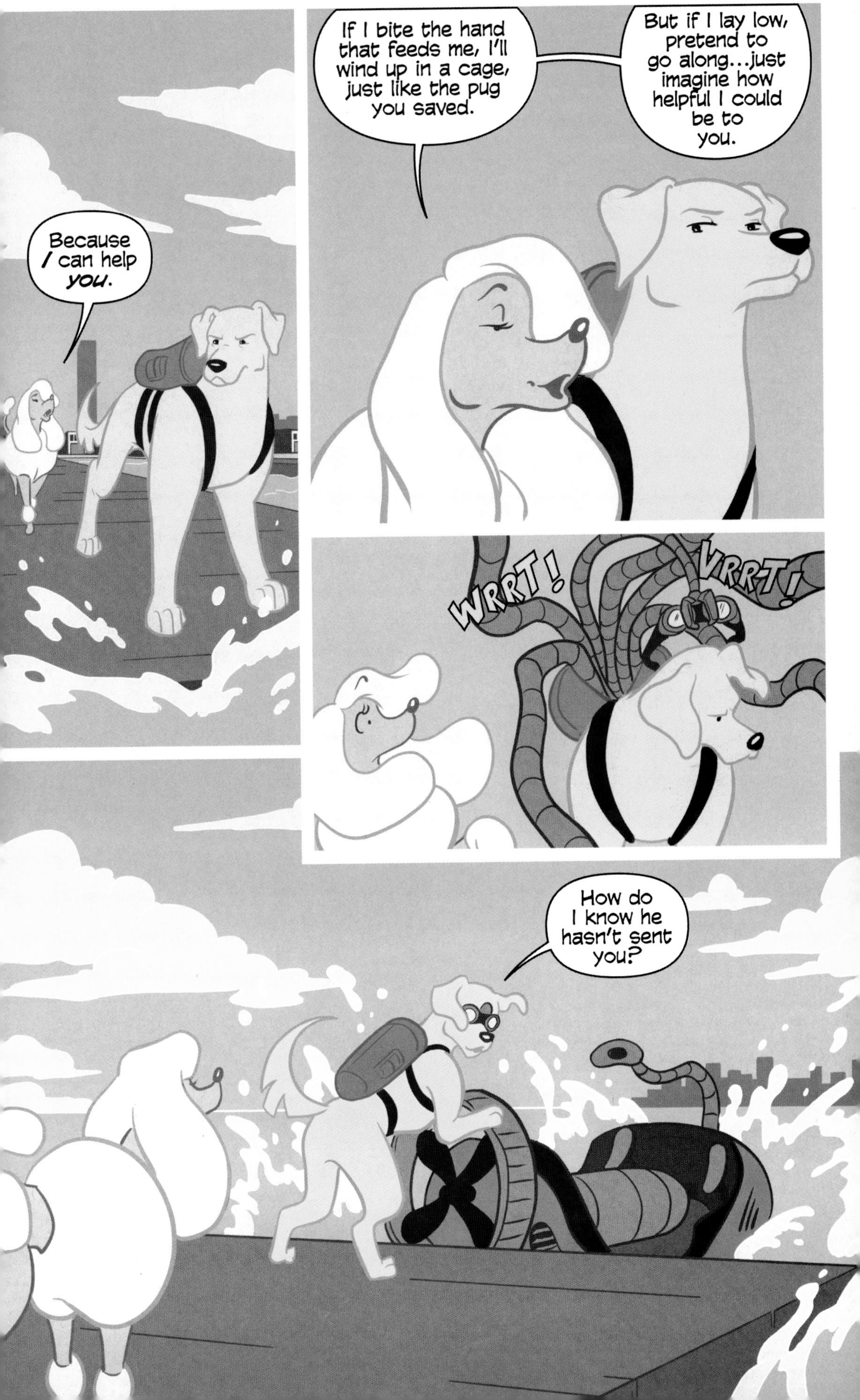

Because *I* can help *you*.
If I bite the hand that feeds me, I'll wind up in a cage, just like the pug you saved.
But if I lay low, pretend to go along...just imagine how helpful I could be to you.
WRRT!
VRRT!
How do I know he hasn't sent you?

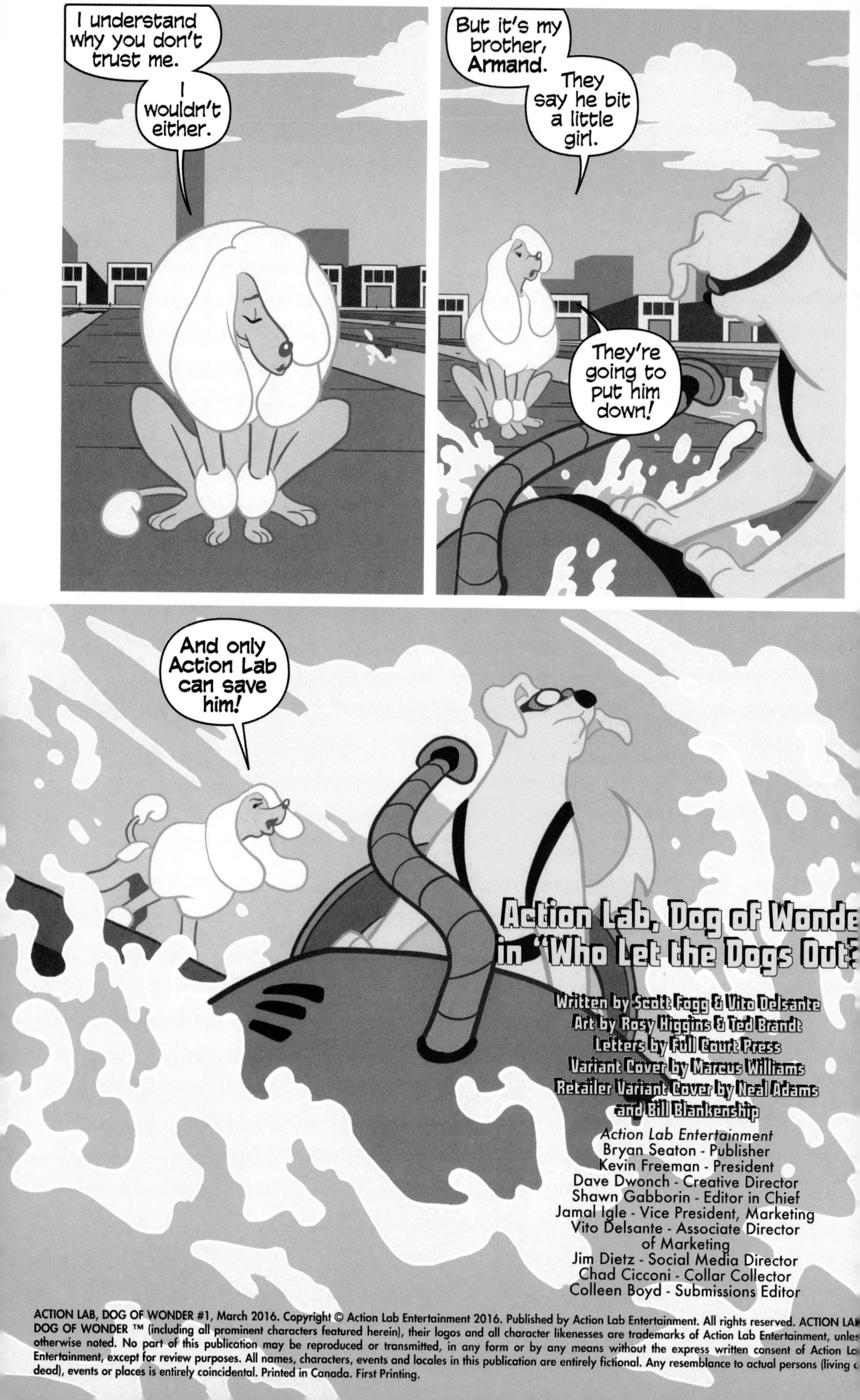
I understand why you don't trust me.
I wouldn't either.
But it's my brother, **Armand**.
They say he bit a little girl.
They're going to put him down!
And only Action Lab can save him!
Action Lab, Dog of Wonde
in "Who Let the Dogs Out?
Written by Scott Fogg & Vito Delsante
Art by Rosy Higgins & Ted Brandt
Letters by Full Court Press
Variant Cover by Marcus Williams
Retailer Variant Cover by Neal Adams and Bill Blankenship
Action Lab Entertainment
Bryan Seaton - Publisher
Kevin Freeman - President
Dave Dwonch - Creative Director
Shawn Gabborin - Editor in Chief
Jamal Igle - Vice President, Marketing
Vito Delsante - Associate Director of Marketing
Jim Dietz - Social Media Director
Chad Cicconi - Collar Collector
Colleen Boyd - Submissions Editor

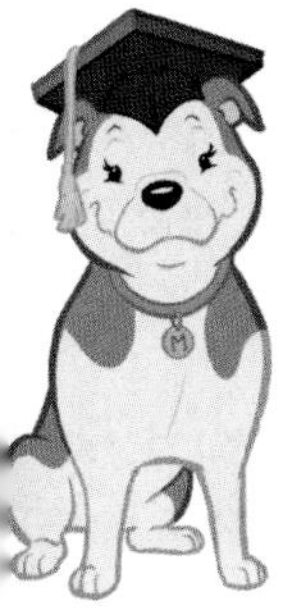

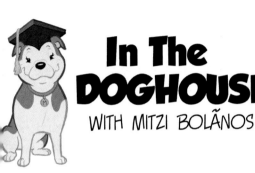

In The DOGHOUSE

WITH MITZI BOLÃNOS

reetings from the Doghouse! I write to you from the ubbyDog headquarters, where our volunteers help ange the negative stereotypes that surround pit bulls. ere is where you'll find answers to common questions on l things dog! If you have other questions, you can email itzibolanos@stubbydog.org.

ogs are so cute! Should I get one?

nimals give us unconditional love and companionship. ey're always there when we need them, and we need be sure we have the time to be there for them. Dogs ed veterinary care like annual checkups and ccasional medicine, healthy food and treats, clean water 4 hours a day, plenty of exercise, play, fun, toys, love, tention, force-free training, baths, brushing, and a soft ed.

on't forget a safe collar, nothing that chokes or pinches e dog, and a good leash. Always walk your dog on a ash, unless you are in a safely fenced area, and never t your dog wander the neighborhood. Your dog should lways wear his ID tags and be microchipped because if e runs away, these things will help you find him quickly.

on't dogs belong in the yard?

ogs love running around outside, but they shouldn't end too much time outside without an adult present, specially on hot summer days, and never during cold inters. If a dog spends time outside in a fenced yard, ake sure he has plenty of water and a safe doghouse. ever leave a dog on a chain. Chained dogs are lonely nd exposed to harsh weather conditions, and they can ven injure or strangle themselves on their chains. Remember, dogs are family, and family lives inside!

hould I go to the pet store, a local breeder, or my local nimal shelter for a dog?

ven though there aren't enough homes for all the uppies born each year, breeders continue to breed for et stores. Thousands of dogs die every single day in merican animal shelters simply because they have owhere to go. A majority of these dogs are pit bulls. By oing to your local animal shelter to adopt your next dog, ou are saving a life, and you'll never regret it. Remember, you don't need to adopt a puppy in order to "raise im right." Adult dogs, of any breed, make fun and sweet ompanions. You can find all types of dogs in shelters, om puppies to seniors and purebreds to mutts. When ou save a shelter dog, they'll never forget it.

o I have to train a dog?

raining is a great way to bond with your dog and it's nportant to build a strong relationship based on trust, never on fear. Never hit, shock, or otherwise scare or hurt your dog to teach him a lesson.

Why do dogs bite?

Dogs can bite because they are scared or have been startled, or if they feel threatened. They can bite to protect something that is valuable to them, like their puppies, their food or a toy.

Dogs who have to live on a chain are the most likely to bite someone. You may think because they are restrained they are not a danger, but dogs that spend their lives on chains are not socialized to be with people. They become frightened and feel trapped, which leads to biting.

What if I have a little brother or sister?

Always teach younger kids to respect animals. Never tease dogs by taking their toys, food or treats, or by pretending to hit or kick. When a dog is eating, give him space, and when a dog goes to sleep, let him rest peacefully. Avoid yelling, running, hitting or making sudden movements toward dogs. Respect their space. If a dog seems uncomfortable by you, be a tree, meaning stop moving and stand still.

What about pit bulls? Aren't they supposed to be aggressive?

Any dog can be aggressive. Did you know that the bloodhound, the bulldog, and the German shepherd were considered aggressive in the 1800s and 1900s? There is nothing in pit bull DNA that makes these dogs any more aggressive than other breeds. Pit bulls actually serve as search and rescue dogs, police dogs, therapy dogs, and emotional support dogs. They live happy and peaceful lives with all sorts of companions, including kids, other dogs, and cats.

Do pit bulls like to fight?

Dogs do not fight voluntarily and dogfighting is not natural. It takes months and years of torture and abuse in order to make these dogs fight. Dogfighting is cruel, illegal, and causes dogs to suffer terribly every day.

Why do people make pit bulls fight?

Sometimes people choose to raise loveable dogs, such as pit bulls, for the wrong reasons. People torture these dogs to make them fight, or use harsh training methods to turn them into guard dogs. When treated this way, dogs can become fearful of people. This doesn't mean they're bad dogs, and if rescued, they can become great family dogs.

People use their dogs to fight in order to make money and to boost their own image, but this doesn't make them tough or cool. These people are only cowards. Real fighters, including celebrities from all types of human fighting associations like the WWE (World Wrestling Entertainment), UFC (Ultimate Fighting Championship), and MMA (mixed martial arts) have taken a stand against dogfighting.

What is a bait dog?

Bait dogs are part of the cruel training involved in dogfighting. They are usually tied up and have their teeth filed down so that they are unable to fight back.

For more information, visit StubbyDog.org!

What can happen to someone for attending a dogfight?

Fighting dogs is a felony in all 50 states, and it is even a crime to attend and watch a dogfight. There are serious consequences for taking part in dogfighting, including jail time.

When dogfighters go to jail, what happens to the dogs?

Even formerly abused dogs forced to fight have been rehabilitated to become loving family pets and even therapy dogs who visit schools and hospitals! Remember, "you are not defined by your scars."

What would *Action Lab* do if he saw...

... a dog constantly on a chain?

Some areas have laws about keeping dogs on a chain. Contact local police and animal control and let them know what you saw. We should treat our dogs the way we want to be treated, with plenty of food, water, attention, love, and fun.

... a dog with scars?

Don't judge! Not all dogs with scars came from a fighting situation. Sometimes strays fight for food on the street, or get stuck trying to dig under or jump over fences. Dogs with scars can be just as sweet and loving as other dogs. However, if you suspect that the dog is being harmed by people, alert your local police and animal control.

... someone hurting a dog?

ALWAYS alert police and animal control if you see someone abusing or neglecting a dog. We have to be their voice. They're counting on us.

... someone talking about dogfighting?

ALWAYS alert police and animal control if you suspect dog fighting or animal abuse. You could be saving a life. You can also report dogfighting anonymously by calling 1-877-TIP-HSUS.

StubbyDog™
Rediscover the pit bull.

Hey Everyone! Vito and Scott her We're really excited to bring you th new adventures of Percy, the Actio Lab, and all his friends, but we wa YOU to join in on the fun!

First off, we want YOUR fan art! Dra Action Lab or any of his friends (you meet them next month)! Also...do yo have an "action lab" in your life Maybe a you have a pugnacious pug Or a dashing dachshund! Whateve dog you call your best friend, we wa to meet him/her! Tell us why YOUR do is a "dog of wonder!" Send us pics o your pup and maybe your dog will en up on our cover! Email us o PercyTheDogOfWonder@gmail.com And if you just want to talk to an member of the Action Lab League o ask them any questions, you can send to Percy above! He'll be sure to sen them your message!

Next month, we'll announce a new con test, so be sure to come back!

- Scott and Vito!

NEXT ISSUE: You've met Action Lab...now meet the ACTION LAB LEAGUE! The ALL dogs take Marguerite's case...but it's not all it's cracked up to be! Also, how far will Clancy go to stop Action Lab? Come back for Issue Two!

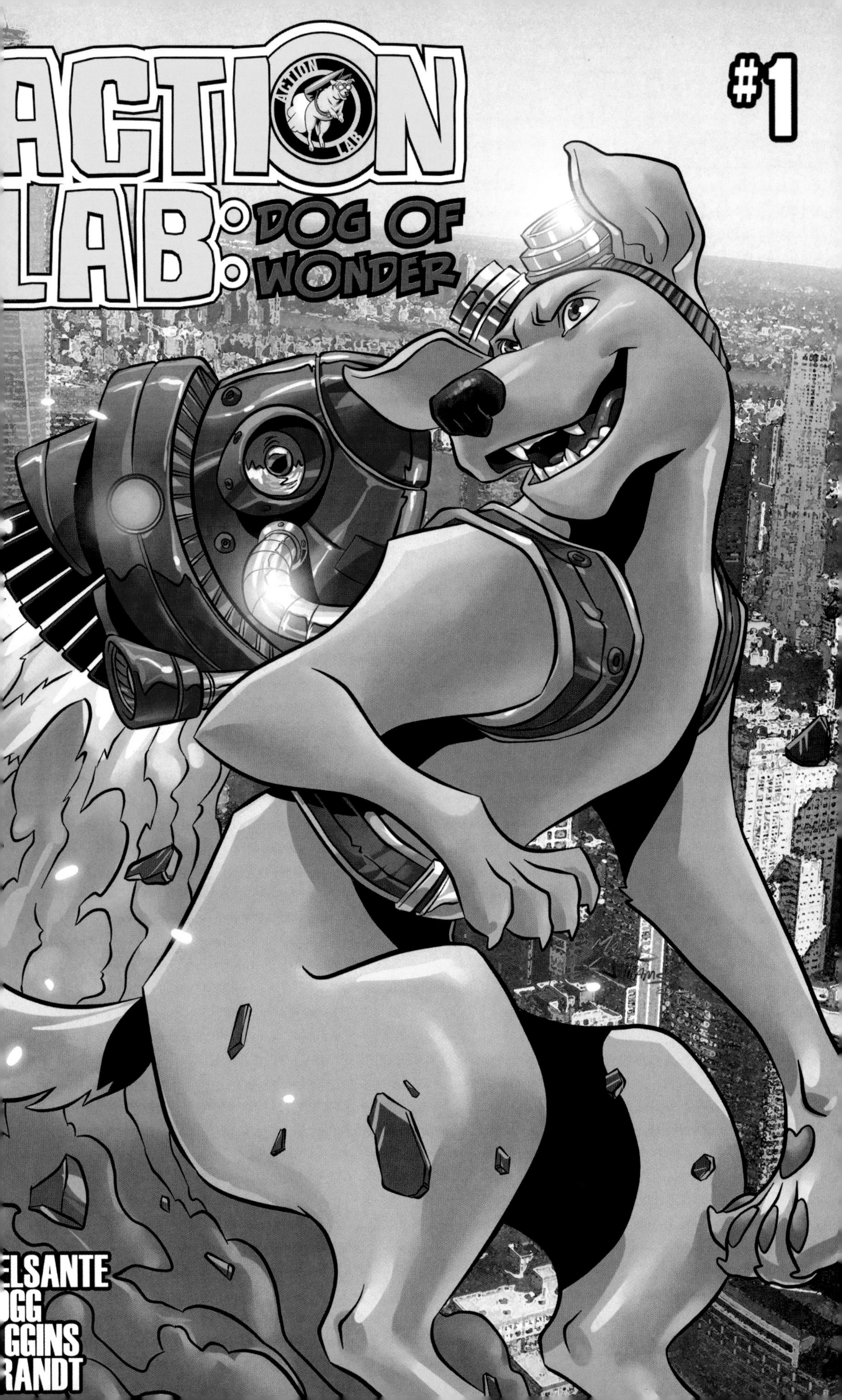

ACTION LAB: DOG OF WONDER
ACTION LAB
#1
ELSANTE
GG
GGINS
RANDT

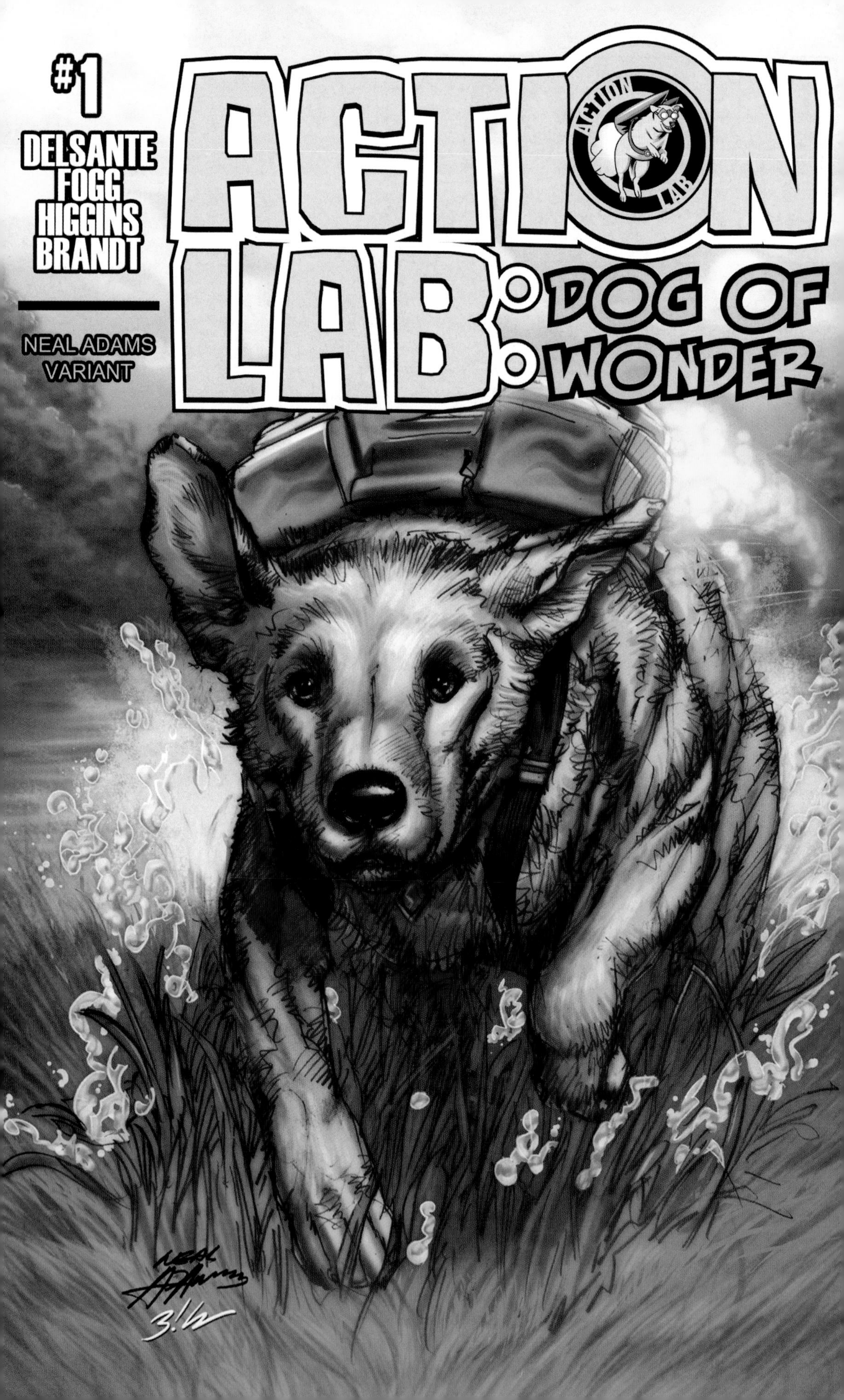
#1
DELSANTE
FOGG
HIGGINS
BRANDT
NEAL ADAMS
VARIANT
ACTION LAB: DOG OF WONDER
ACTION LAB

#1

LSANTE
FOGG
IGGINS
RANDT

AL ADAMS
OLORING
BOOK
VARIANT

ACTION LAB: DOG OF WONDER

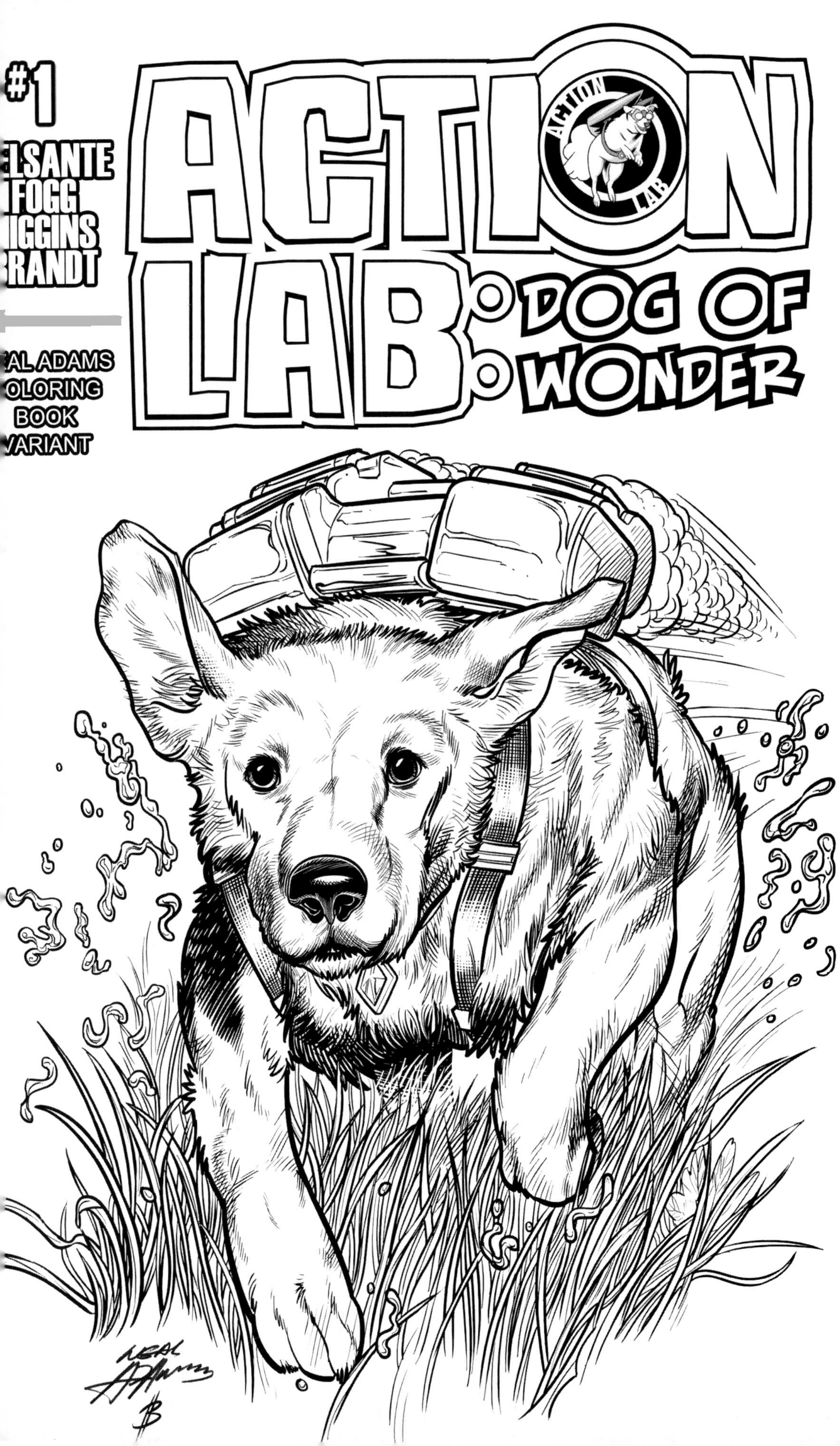

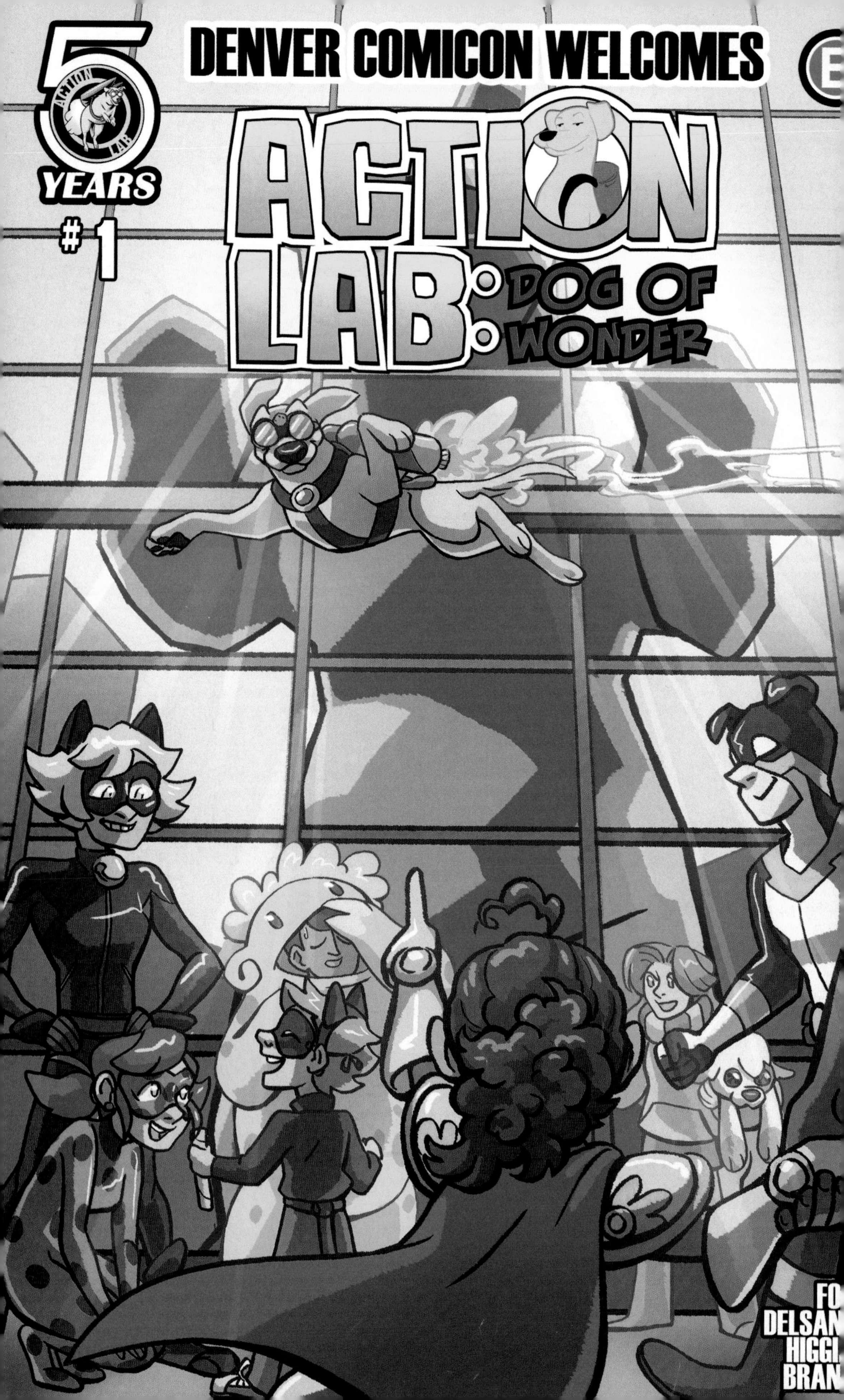

5 YEARS
ACTION LAB
#1
DENVER COMICON WELCOMES
ACTION LAB: DOG OF WONDER
FO
DELSAN
HIGGI
BRAN

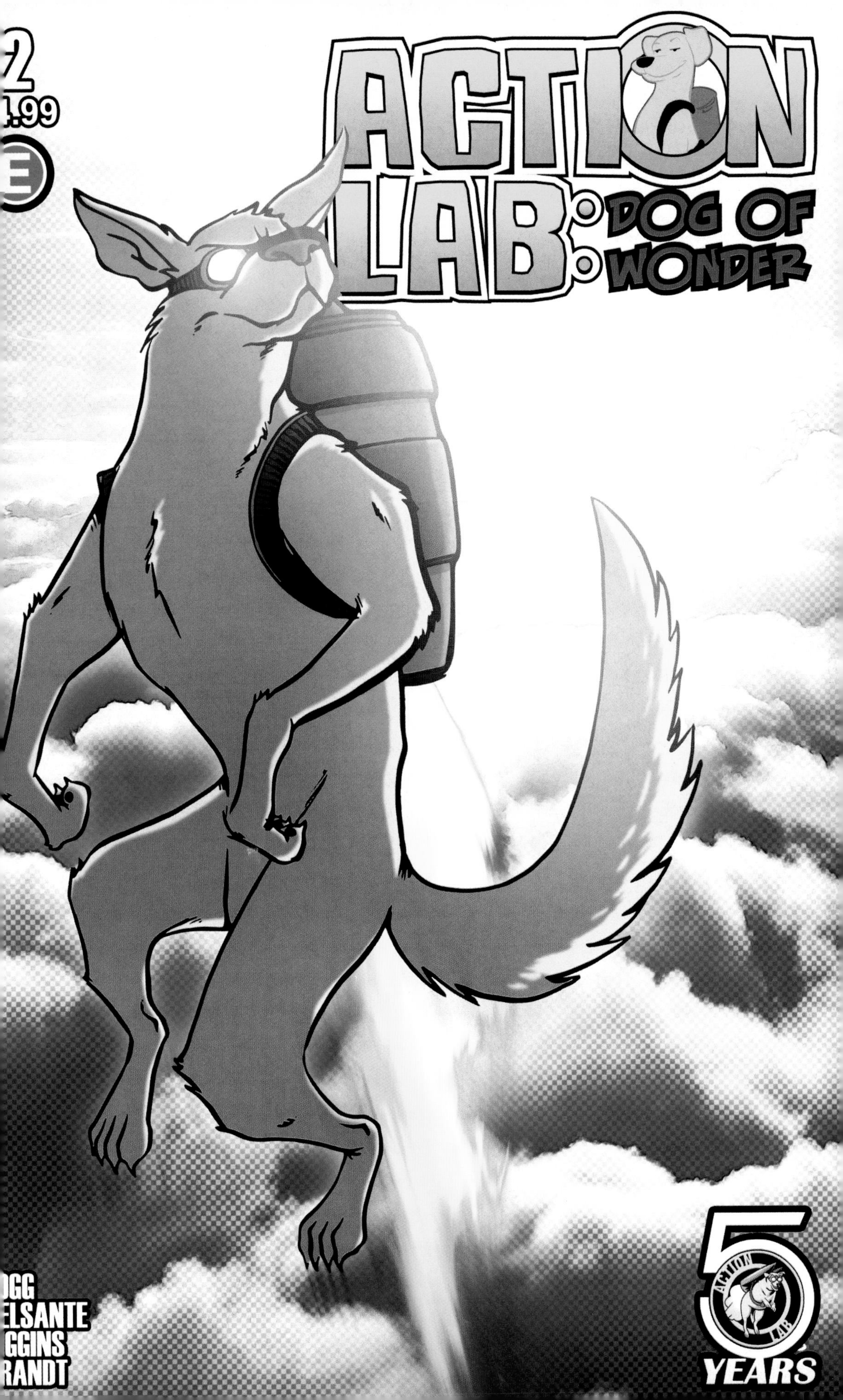
2
.99
ACTION LAB: DOG OF WONDER
OGG
ELSANTE
GGINS
RANDT
5 YEARS
ACTION LAB

READ MORE NOW

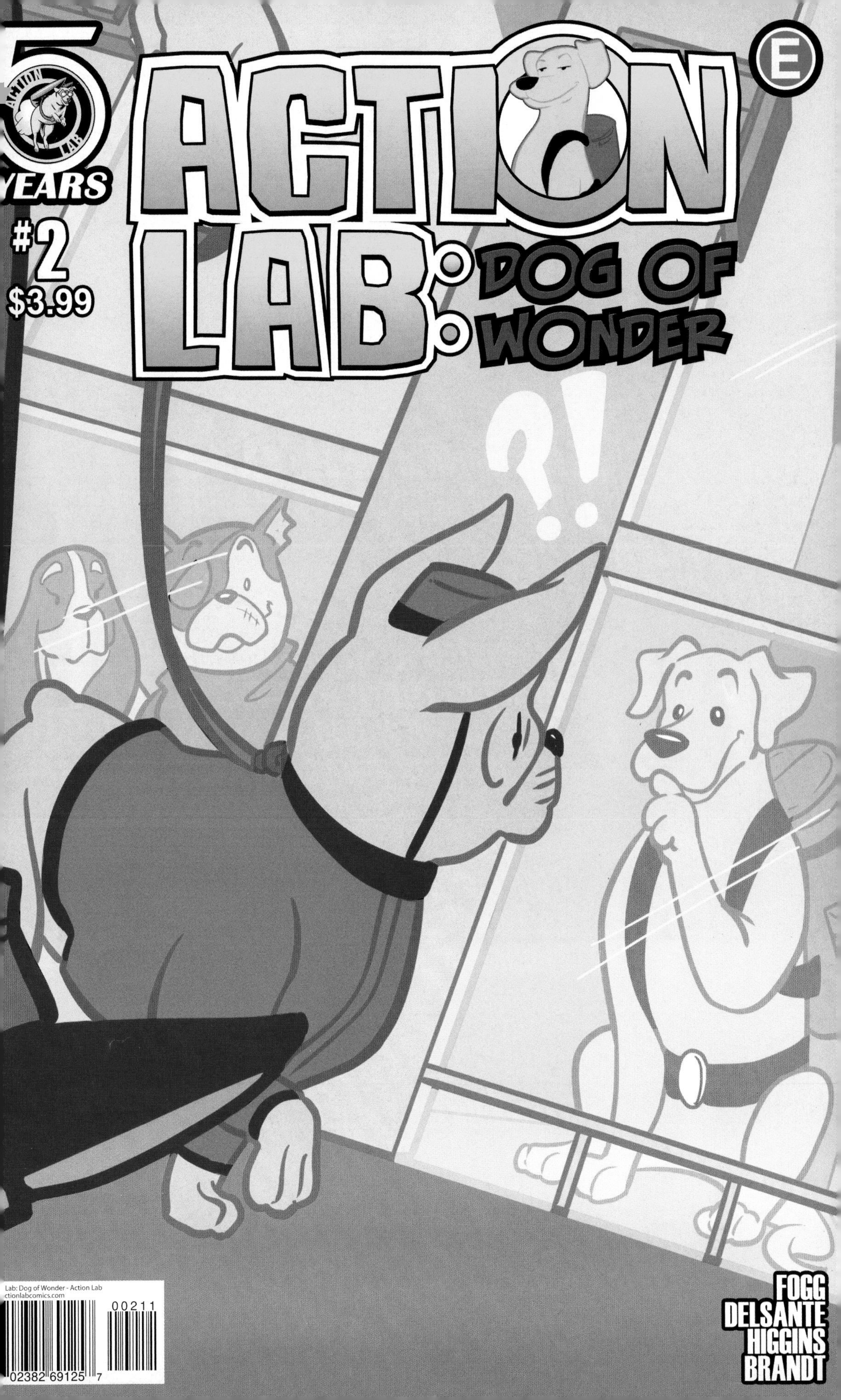
5 YEARS
ACTION LAB
#2
$3.99
E
ACTION LAB: DOG OF WONDER
?!
FOGG
DELSANTE
HIGGINS
BRANDT
Lab: Dog of Wonder - Action Lab
ctionlabcomics.com
00211
02382 69125 7

FROM ALL-AGES TO MATURE READERS
ACTION LAB HAS YOU COVERED.

 **Appropriate for everyone.**

 **Appropriate for age 9 and up. Absent of profanity or adult content.**

 **Suggested for 12 and Up. Comics with this rating are comparable to a PG-13 movie rating. Recommended for our teen and young adult readers.**

 **Appropriate for older teens. Similar to Teen, but featuring more mature themes and/or more graphic imagery.**

 **Contains extreme violence and some nudity. Basically the Rated-R of comics.**

FIND YOUR NEW FAVORITE COMICS.

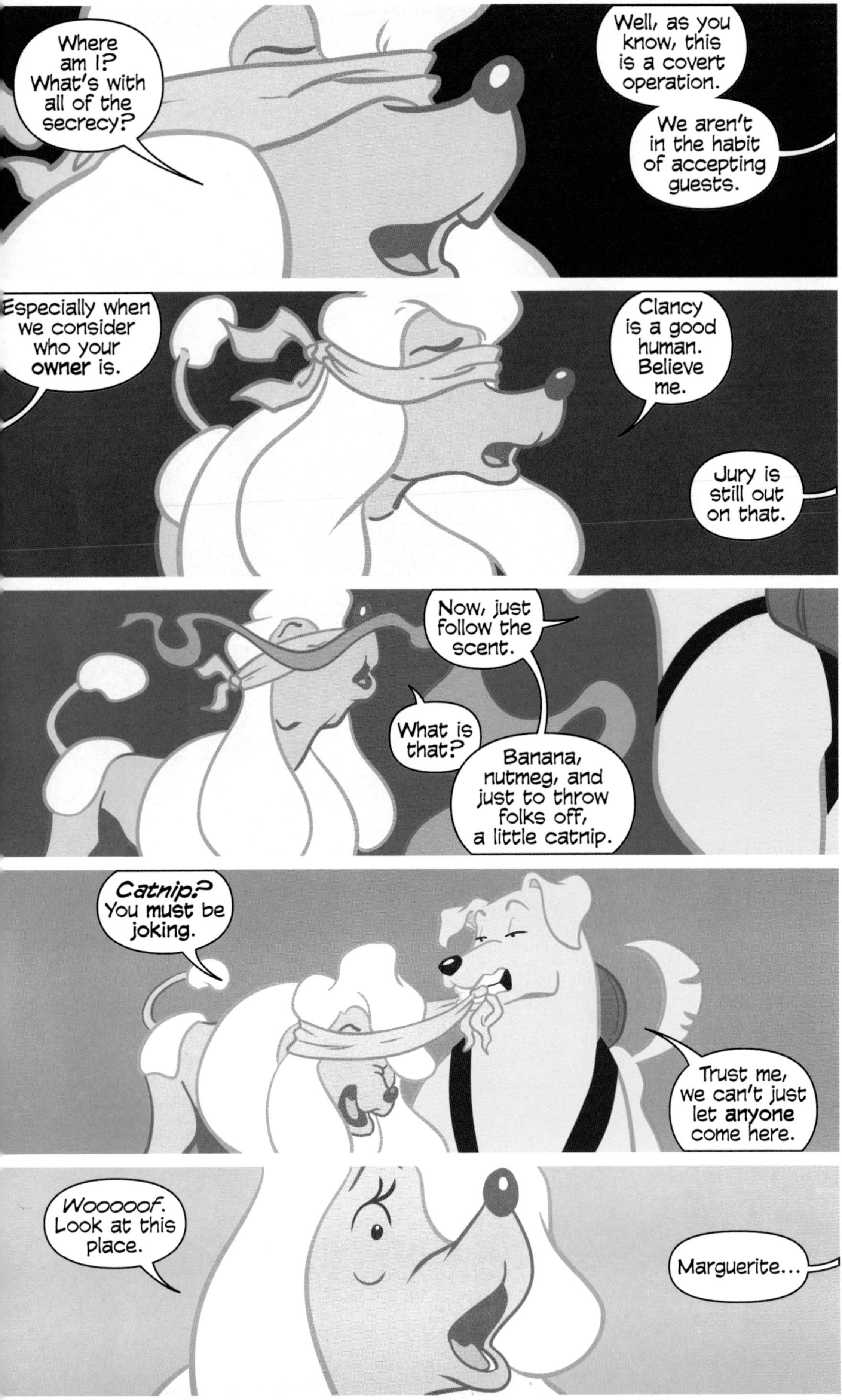

Where am I? What's with all of the secrecy?
Well, as you know, this is a covert operation.
We aren't in the habit of accepting guests.
Especially when we consider who your **owner** is.
Clancy is a good human. Believe me.
Jury is still out on that.
Now, just follow the scent.
What is that?
Banana, nutmeg, and just to throw folks off, a little catnip.
Catnip? You **must** be joking.
Trust me, we can't just let **anyone** come here.
Woooof. Look at this place.
Marguerite...

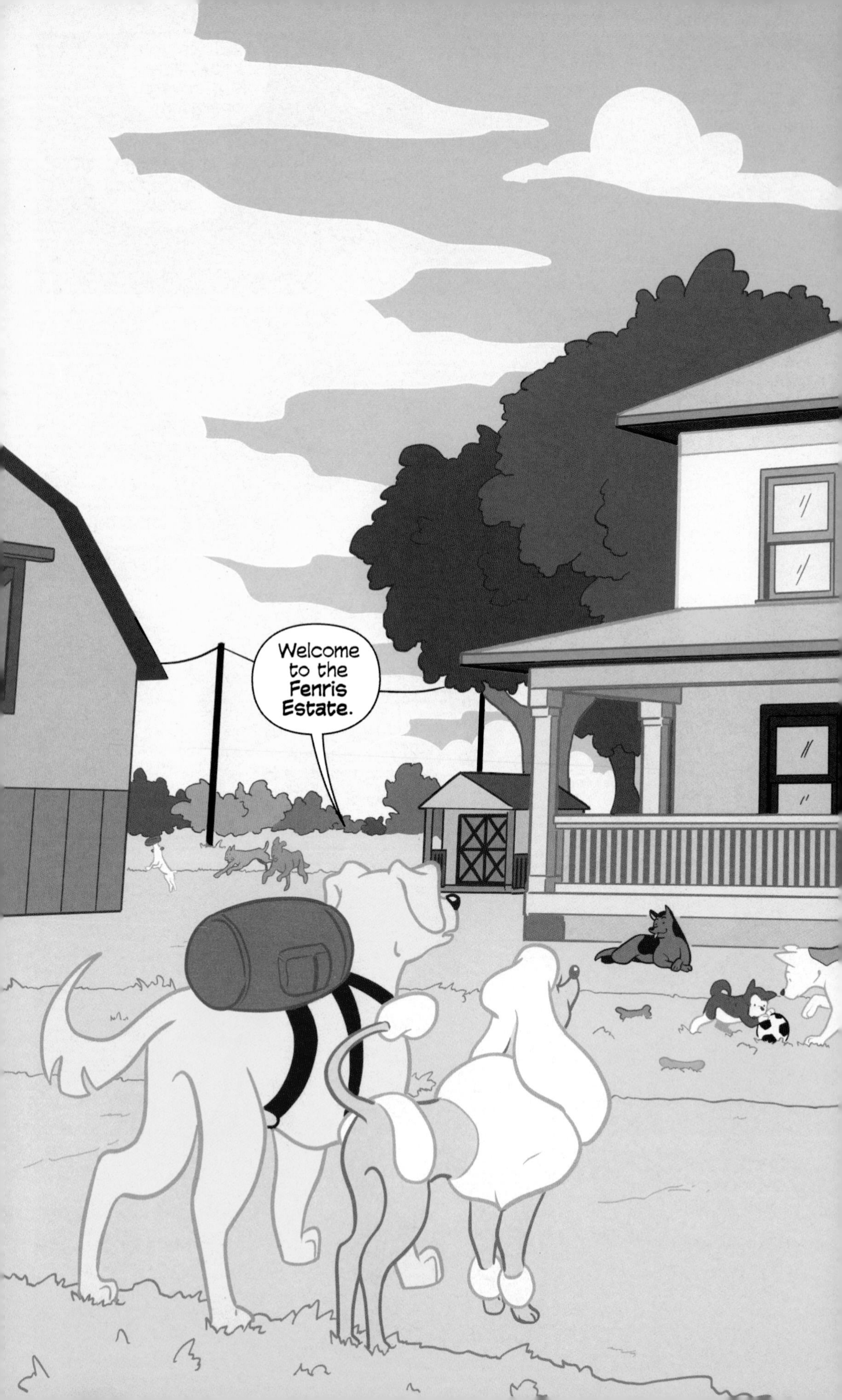
Welcome to the Fenris Estate.

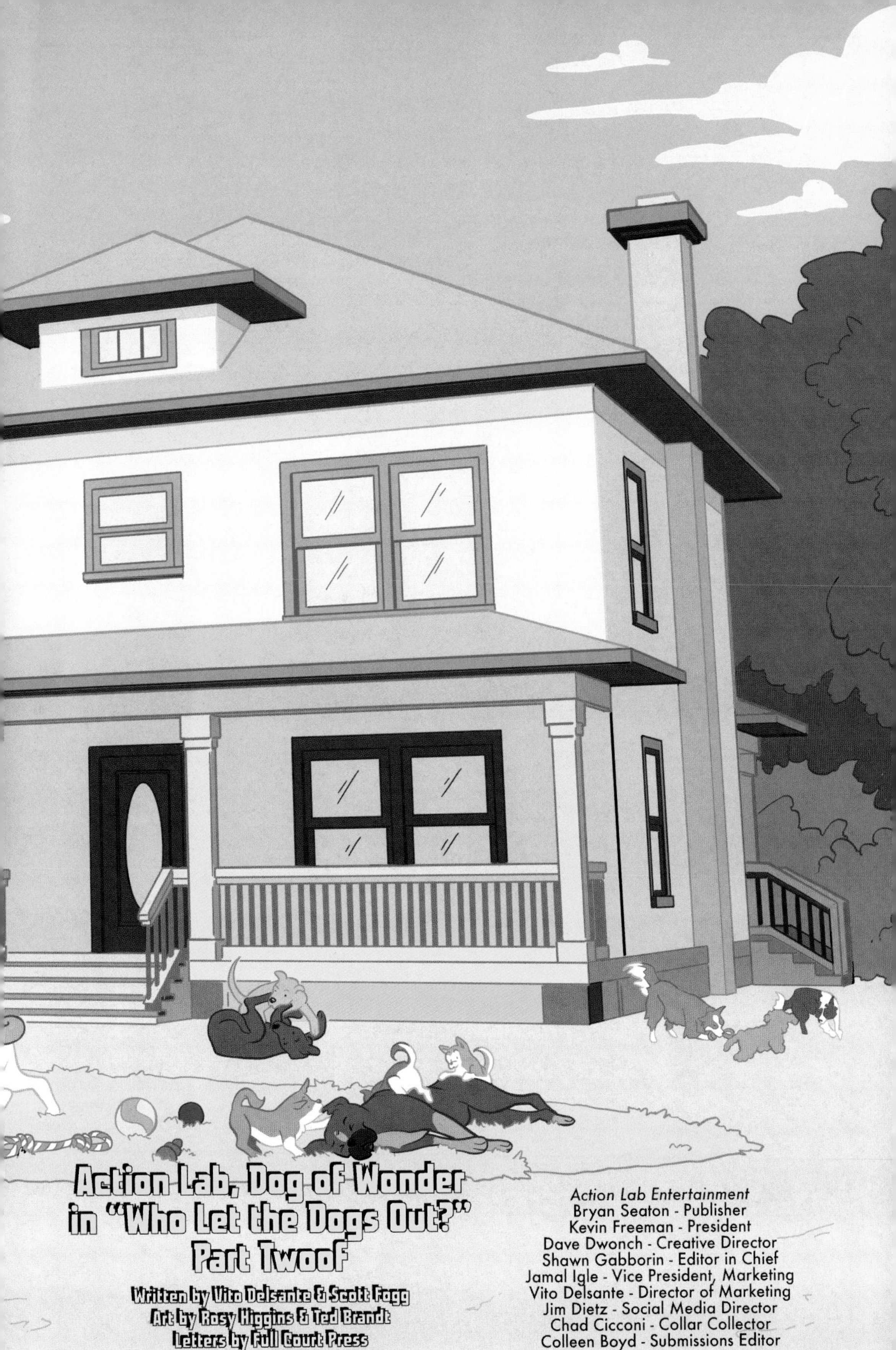

Action Lab, Dog of Wonder in "Who Let the Dogs Out?" Part Twoof

Written by Vito Delsante & Scott Fogg
Art by Rosy Higgins & Ted Brandt
Letters by Full Court Press
Variant Cover by Sam Ellis

Action Lab Entertainment
Bryan Seaton - Publisher
Kevin Freeman - President
Dave Dwonch - Creative Director
Shawn Gabborin - Editor in Chief
Jamal Igle - Vice President, Marketing
Vito Delsante - Director of Marketing
Jim Dietz - Social Media Director
Chad Cicconi - Collar Collector
Colleen Boyd - Submissions Editor

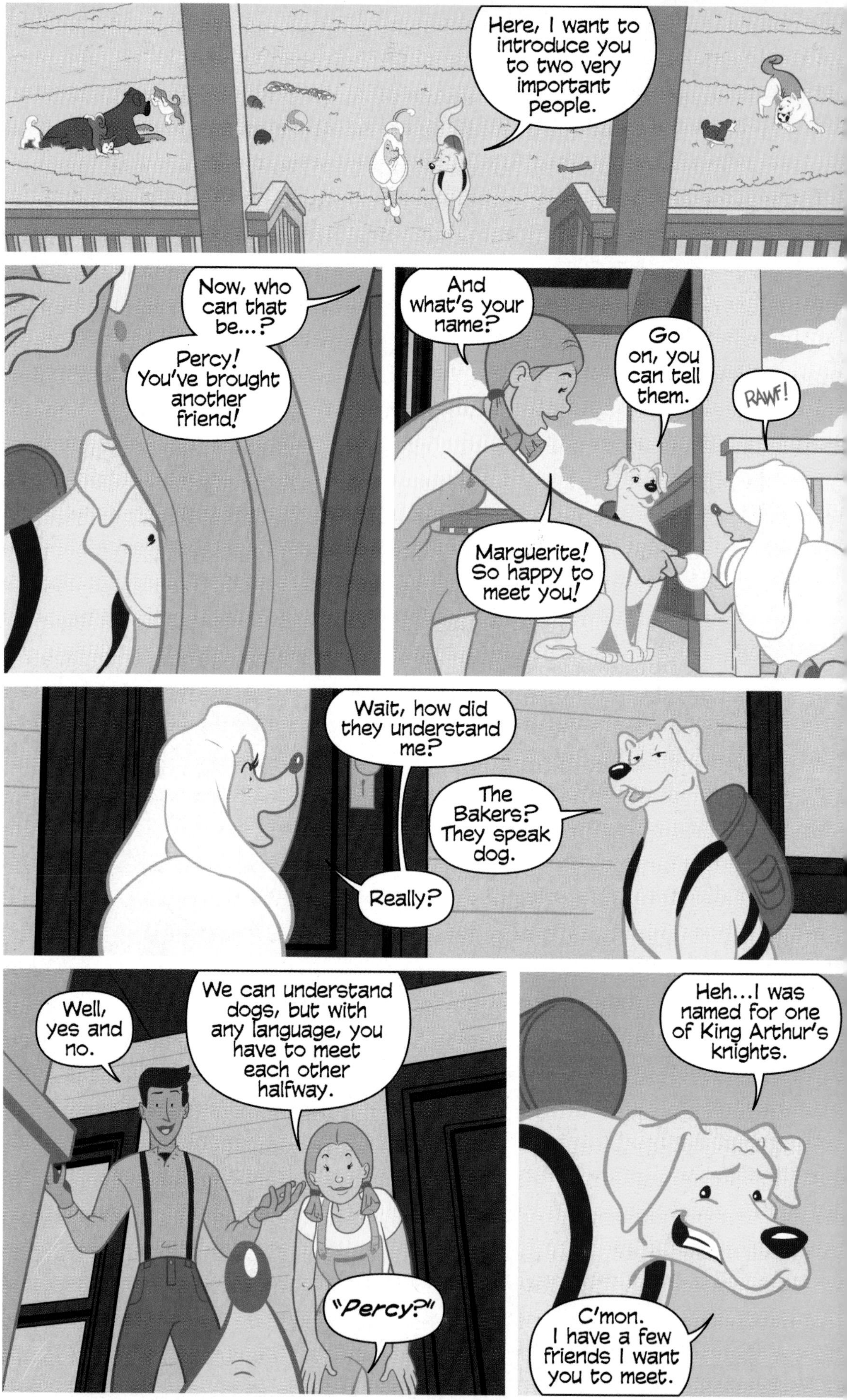

Here, I want to introduce you to two very important people.
Now, who can that be...?
Percy! You've brought another friend!
And what's your name?
Go on, you can tell them.
RAWF!
Marguerite! So happy to meet you!
Wait, how did they understand me?
The Bakers? They speak dog.
Really?
Well, yes and no.
We can understand dogs, but with any language, you have to meet each other halfway.
"Percy?"
Heh...I was named for one of King Arthur's knights.
C'mon. I have a few friends I want you to meet.

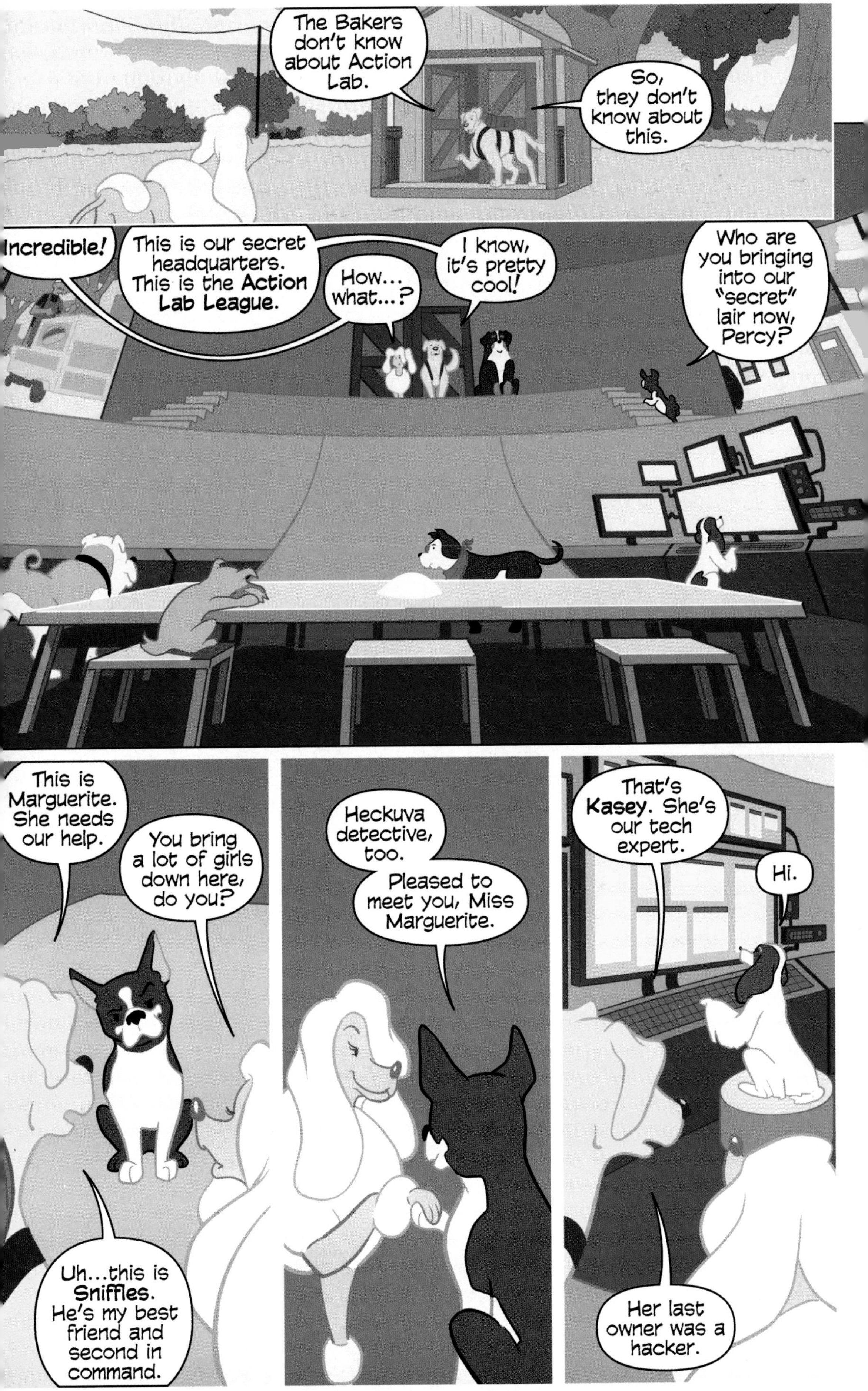
The Bakers don't know about Action Lab.
So, they don't know about this.
Incredible!
This is our secret headquarters. This is the Action Lab League.
How... what...?
I know, it's pretty cool!
Who are you bringing into our "secret" lair now, Percy?
This is Marguerite. She needs our help.
You bring a lot of girls down here, do you?
Uh...this is Sniffles. He's my best friend and second in command.
Heckuva detective, too.
Pleased to meet you, Miss Marguerite.
That's Kasey. She's our tech expert.
Hi.
Her last owner was a hacker.

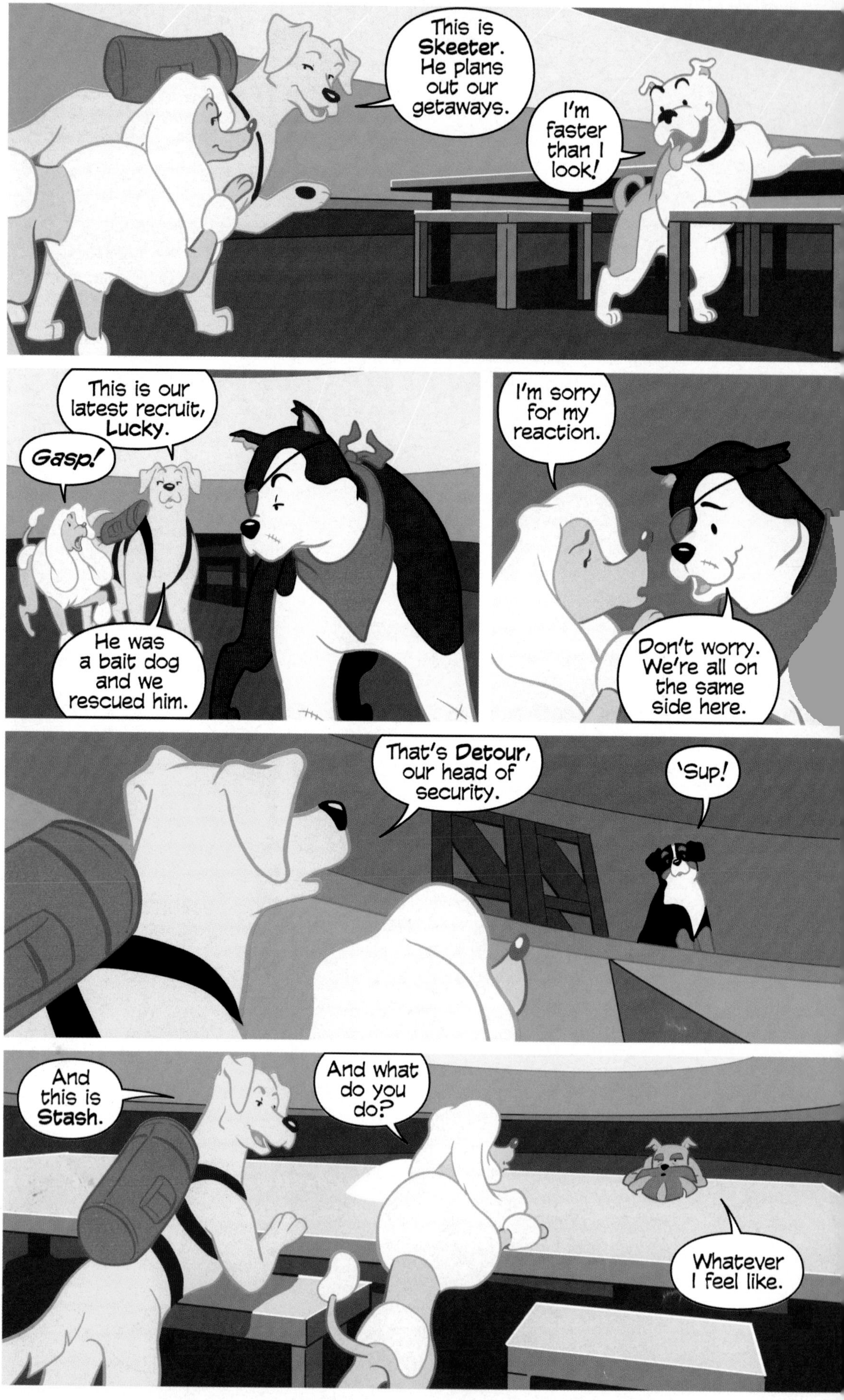
This is Skeeter. He plans out our getaways.
I'm faster than I look!
This is our latest recruit, Lucky.
Gasp!
He was a bait dog and we rescued him.
I'm sorry for my reaction.
Don't worry. We're all on the same side here.
That's Detour, our head of security.
'Sup!
And this is Stash.
And what do you do?
Whatever I feel like.

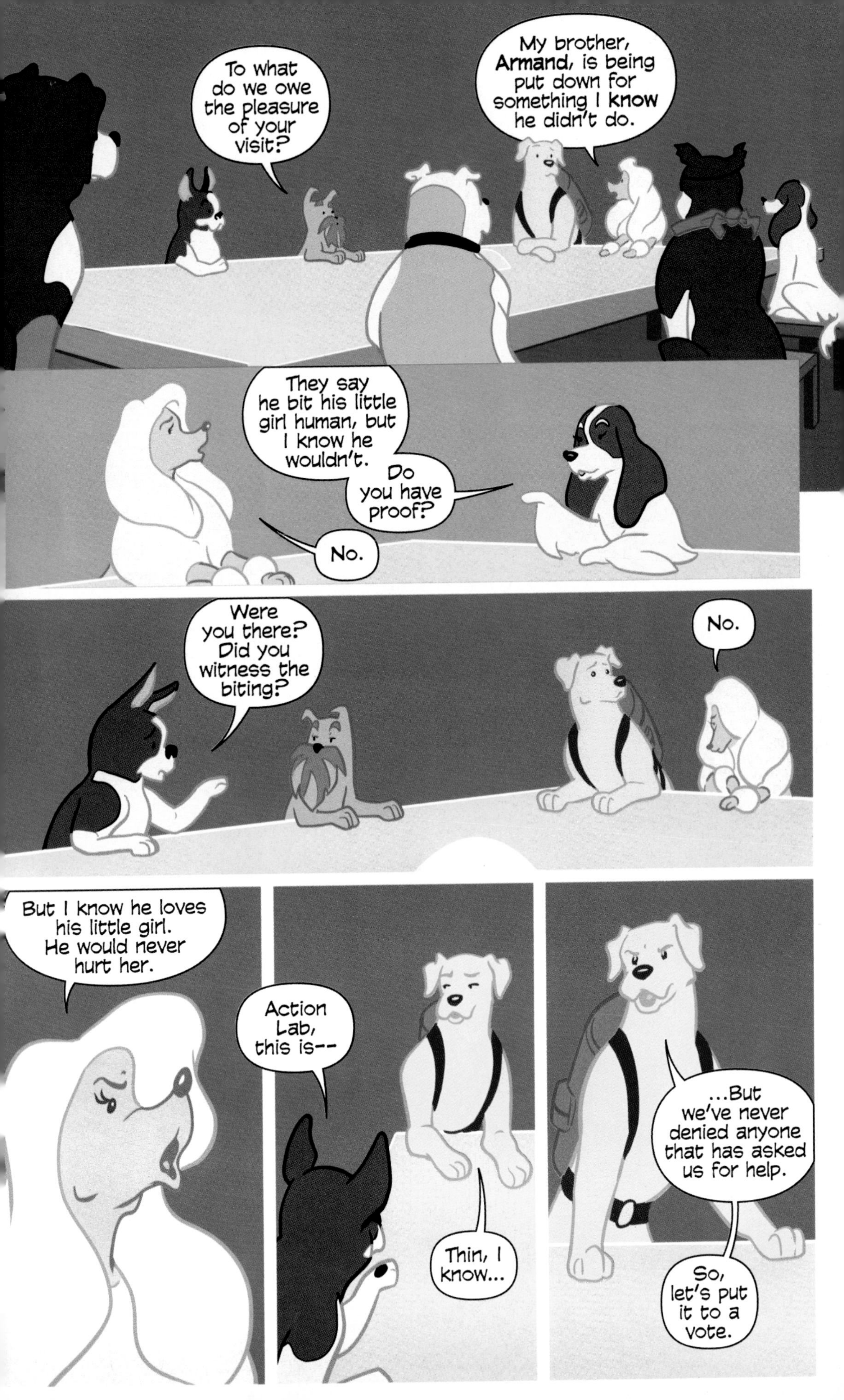
To what do we owe the pleasure of your visit?
My brother, Armand, is being put down for something I know he didn't do.
They say he bit his little girl human, but I know he wouldn't.
Do you have proof?
No.
Were you there? Did you witness the biting?
No.
But I know he loves his little girl. He would never hurt her.
Action Lab, this is--
Thin, I know...
...But we've never denied anyone that has asked us for help.
So, let's put it to a vote.

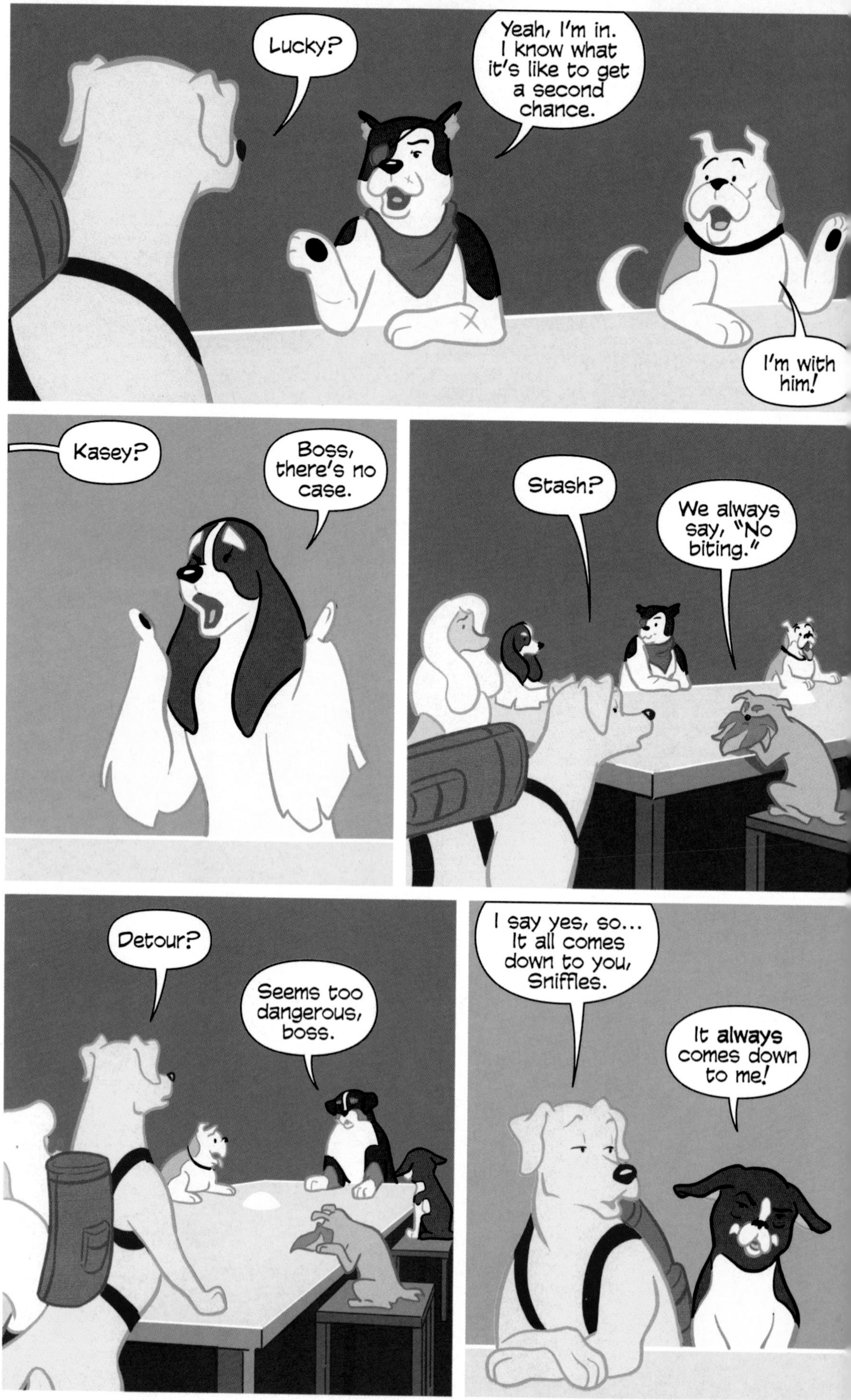
Lucky?
Yeah, I'm in. I know what it's like to get a second chance.
I'm with him!
Kasey?
Boss, there's no case.
Stash?
We always say, "No biting."
Detour?
Seems too dangerous, boss.
I say yes, so... It all comes down to you, Sniffles.
It always comes down to me!

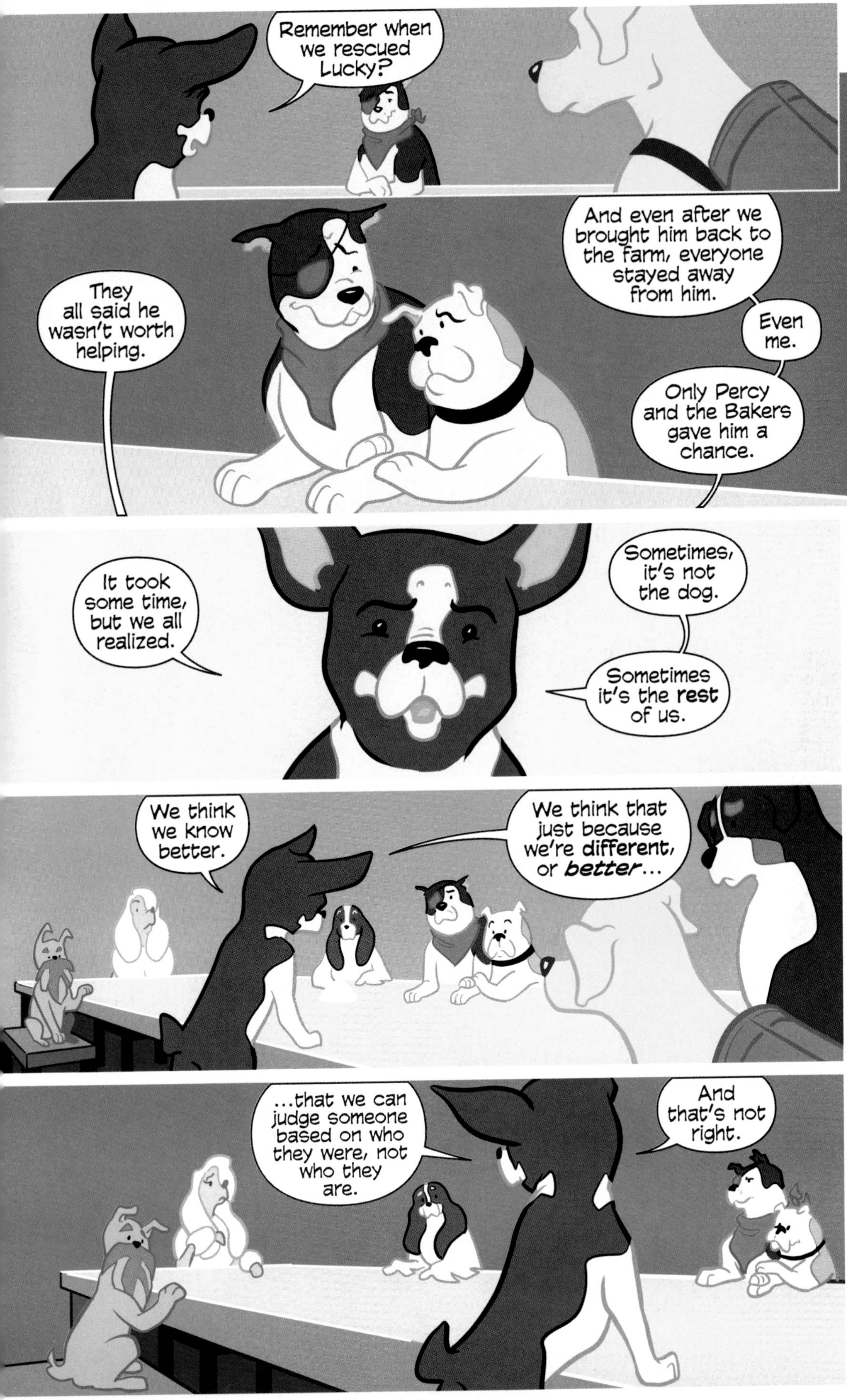

Remember when we rescued Lucky?
They all said he wasn't worth helping.
And even after we brought him back to the farm, everyone stayed away from him.
Even me.
Only Percy and the Bakers gave him a chance.
It took some time, but we all realized.
Sometimes, it's not the dog.
Sometimes it's the **rest** of us.
We think we know better.
We think that just because we're **different**, or ***better***...
...that we can judge someone based on who they were, not who they are.
And that's not right.

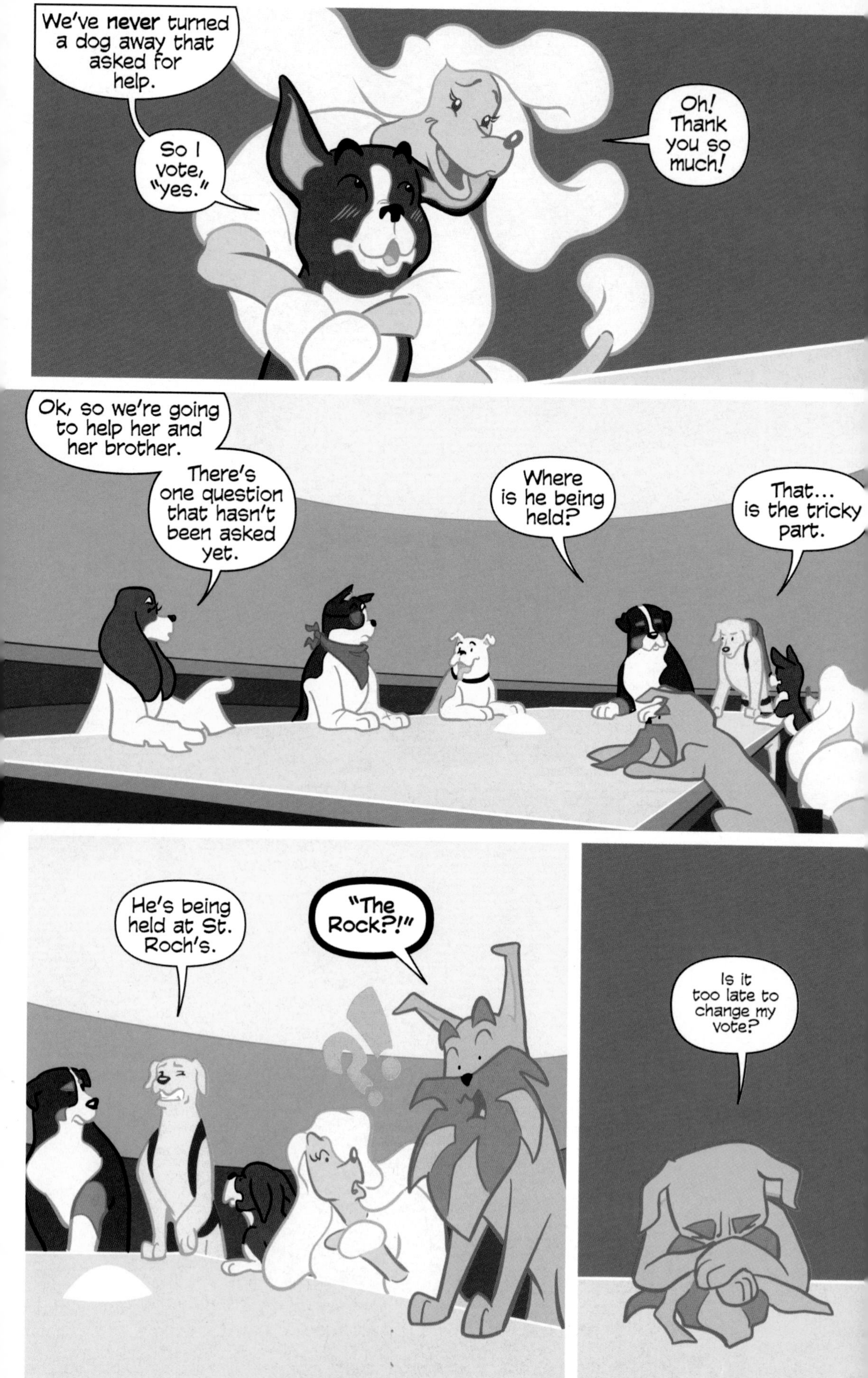
We've **never** turned a dog away that asked for help.
So I vote, "yes."
Oh! Thank you so much!
Ok, so we're going to help her and her brother.
There's one question that hasn't been asked yet.
Where is he being held?
That... is the tricky part.
He's being held at St. Roch's.
"The Rock?!"
Is it too late to change my vote?

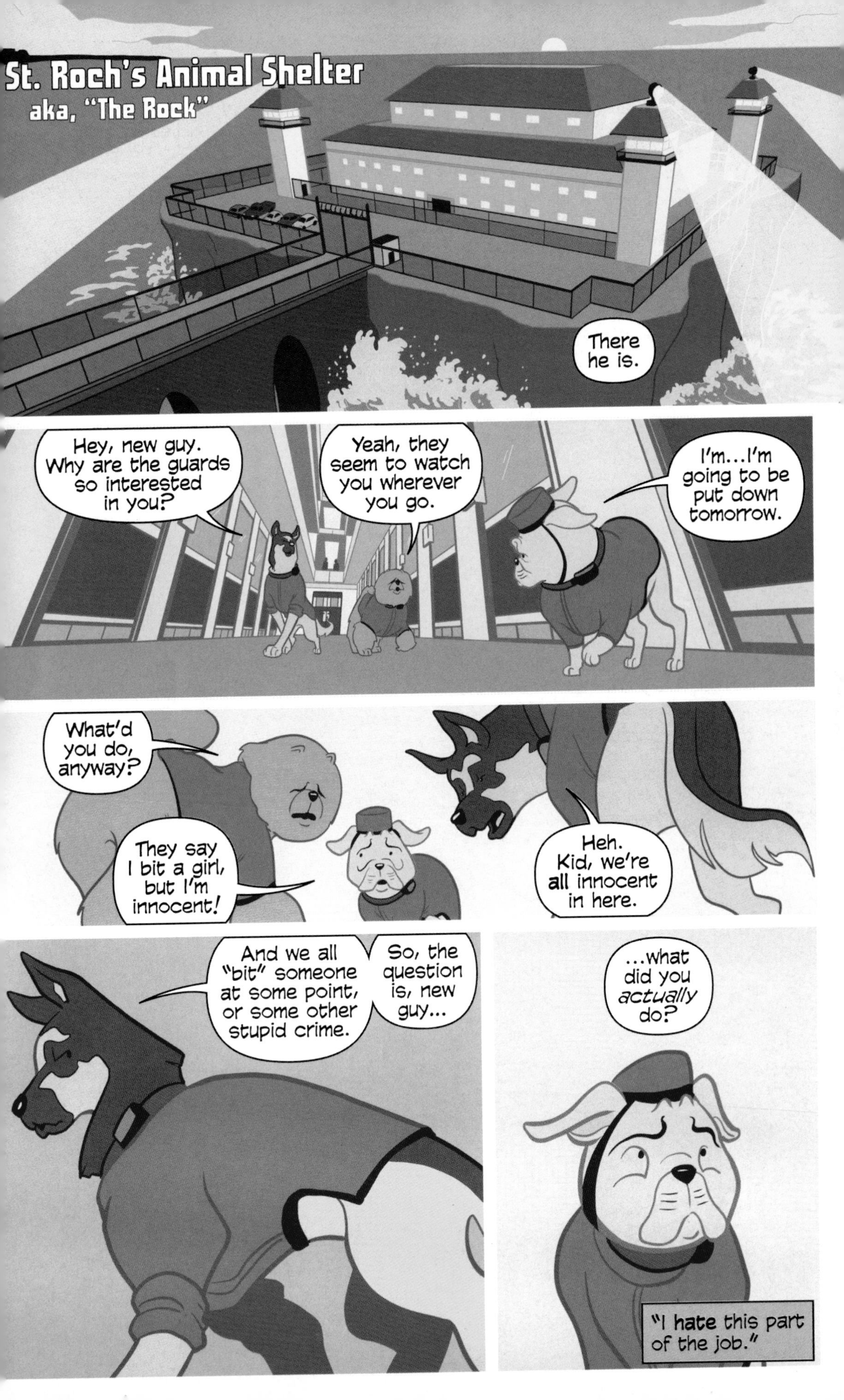
St. Roch's Animal Shelter
aka, "The Rock"
There he is.
Hey, new guy. Why are the guards so interested in you?
Yeah, they seem to watch you wherever you go.
I'm...I'm going to be put down tomorrow.
What'd you do, anyway?
They say I bit a girl, but I'm innocent!
Heh. Kid, we're all innocent in here.
And we all "bit" someone at some point, or some other stupid crime.
So, the question is, new guy...
...what did you actually do?
"I hate this part of the job."

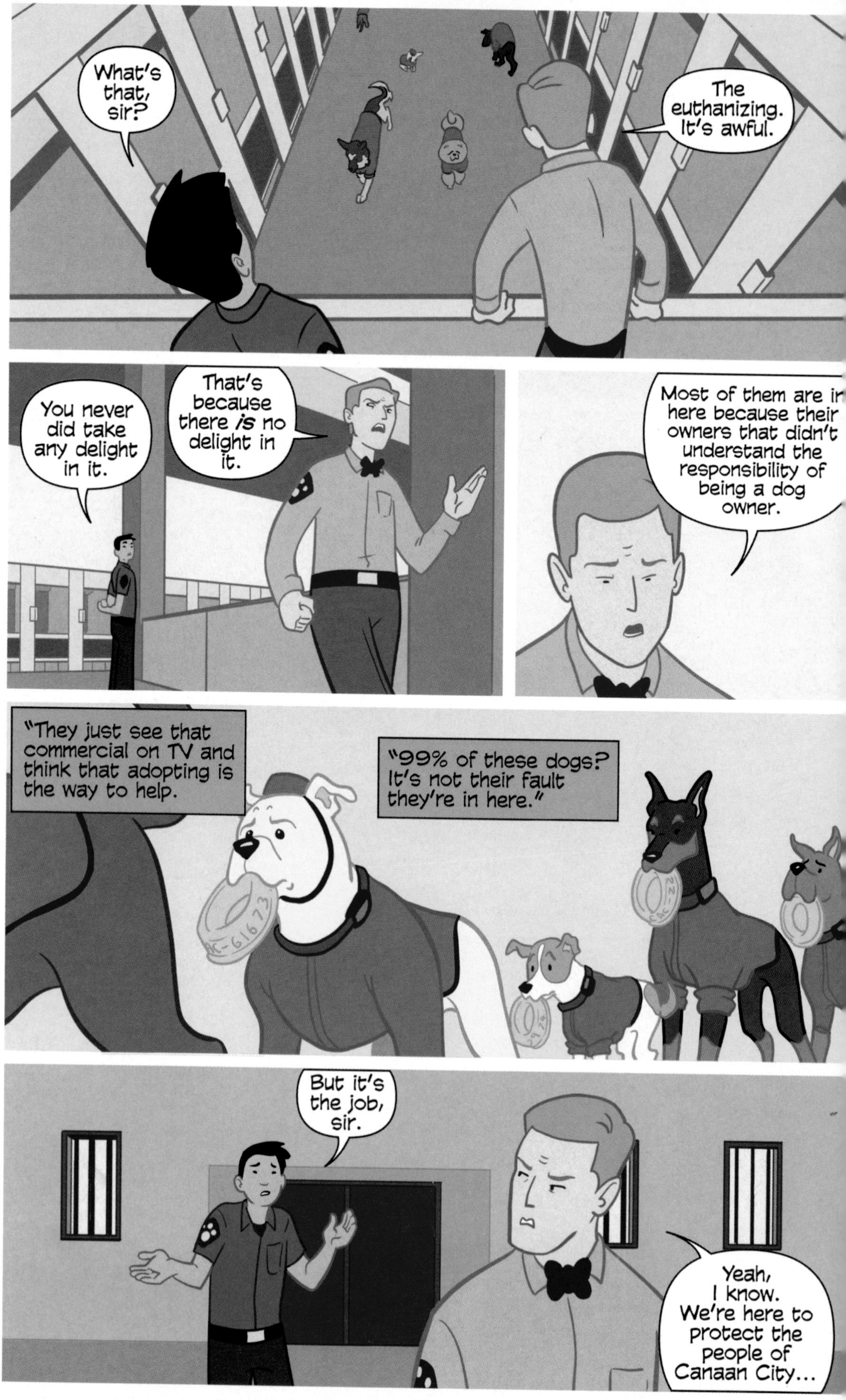

What's that, sir?
The euthanizing. It's awful.
You never did take any delight in it.
That's because there *is* no delight in it.
Most of them are in here because their owners that didn't understand the responsibility of being a dog owner.
"They just see that commercial on TV and think that adopting is the way to help.
"99% of these dogs? It's not their fault they're in here."
But it's the job, sir.
Yeah, I know. We're here to protect the people of Canaan City...

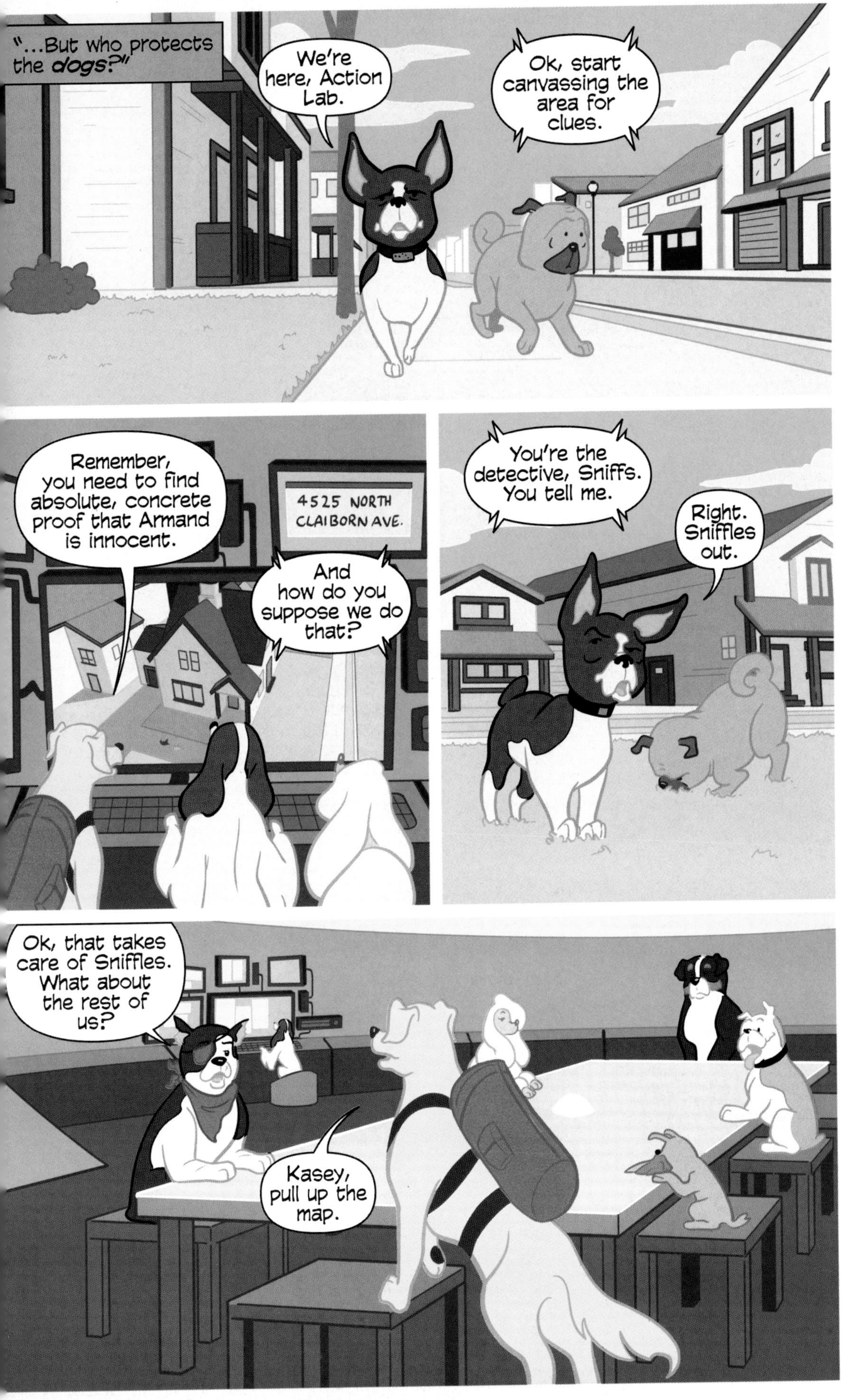
"...But who protects the *dogs?*"
We're here, Action Lab.
Ok, start canvassing the area for clues.
Remember, you need to find absolute, concrete proof that Armand is innocent.
4525 NORTH CLAIBORN AVE.
And how do you suppose we do that?
You're the detective, Sniffs. You tell me.
Right. Sniffles out.
Ok, that takes care of Sniffles. What about the rest of us?
Kasey, pull up the map.

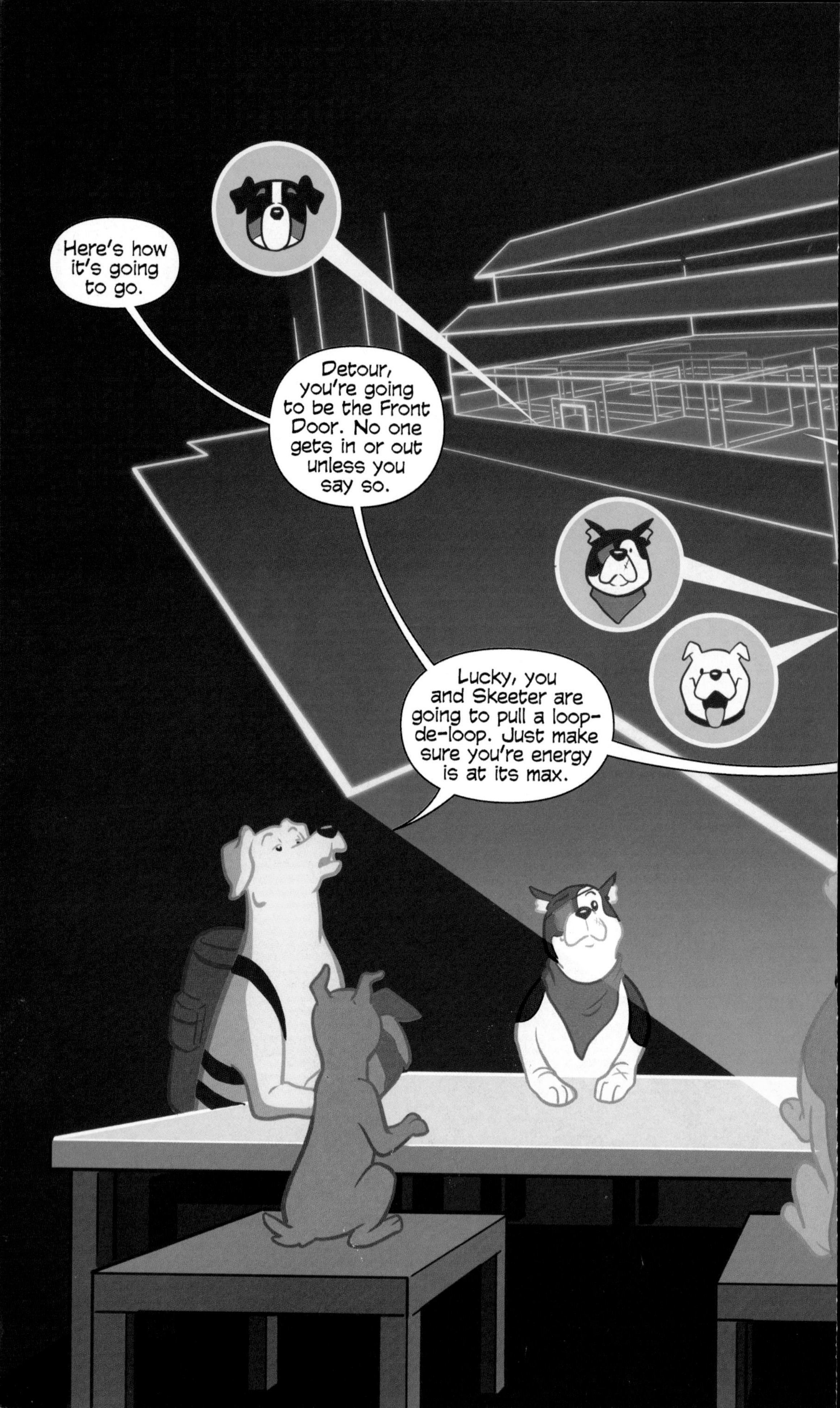
Here's how it's going to go.
Detour, you're going to be the Front Door. No one gets in or out unless you say so.
Lucky, you and Skeeter are going to pull a loop-de-loop. Just make sure you're energy is at its max.

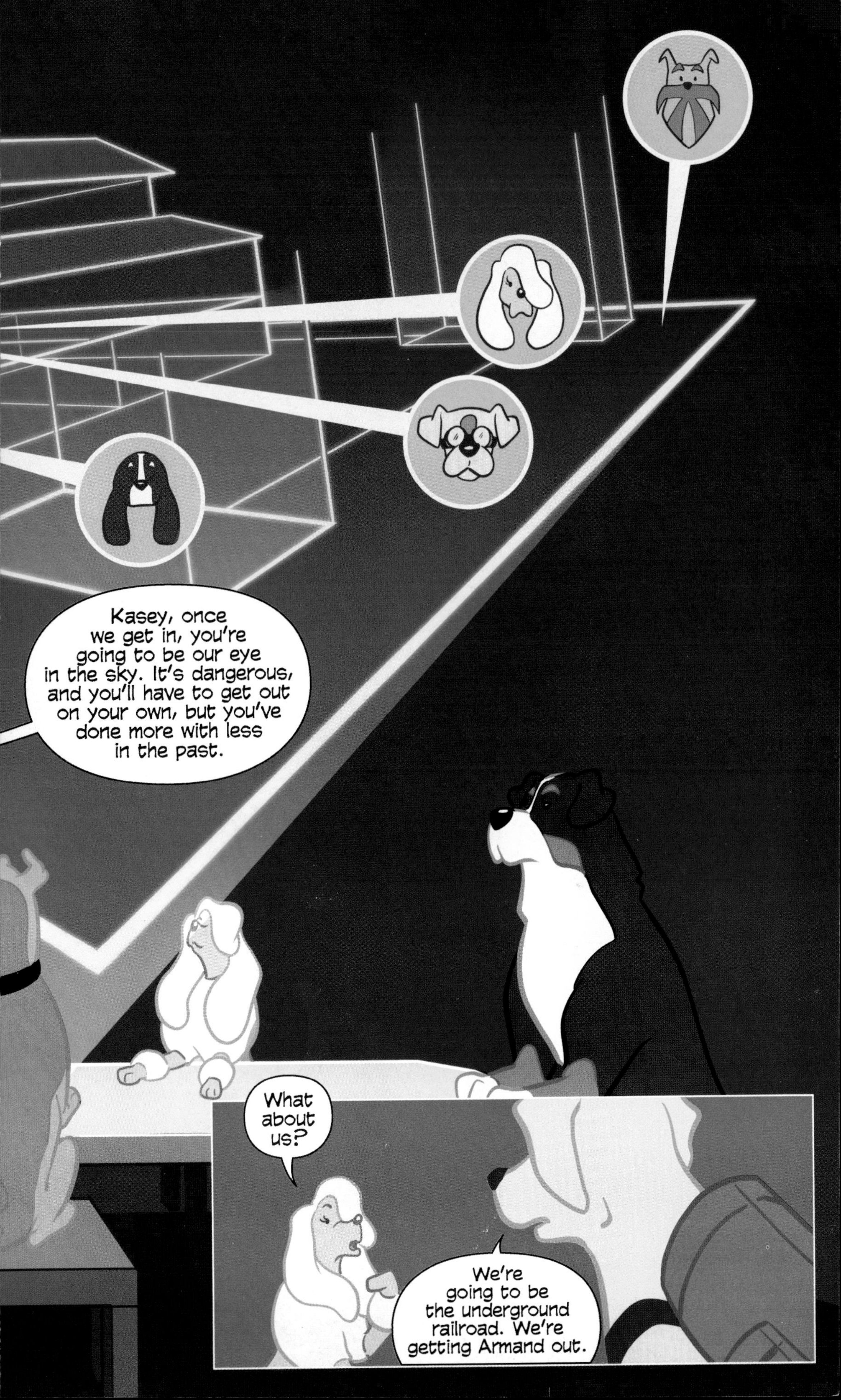

Kasey, once we get in, you're going to be our eye in the sky. It's dangerous, and you'll have to get out on your own, but you've done more with less in the past.
What about us?
We're going to be the underground railroad. We're getting Armand out.

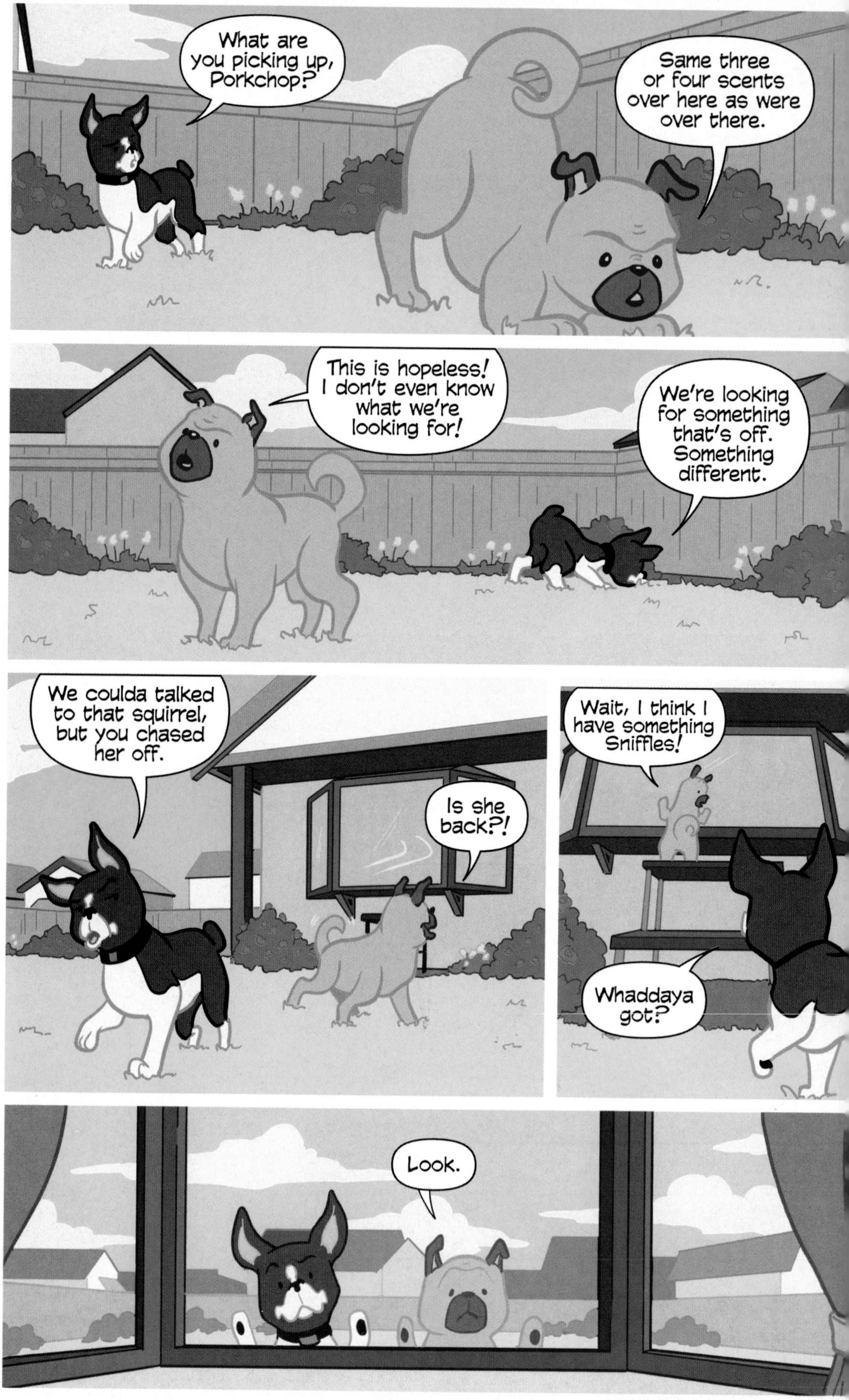
What are you picking up, Porkchop?
Same three or four scents over here as were over there.
This is hopeless! I don't even know what we're looking for!
We're looking for something that's off. Something different.
We coulda talked to that squirrel, but you chased her off.
Is she back?!
Wait, I think I have something Sniffles!
Whaddaya got?
Look.

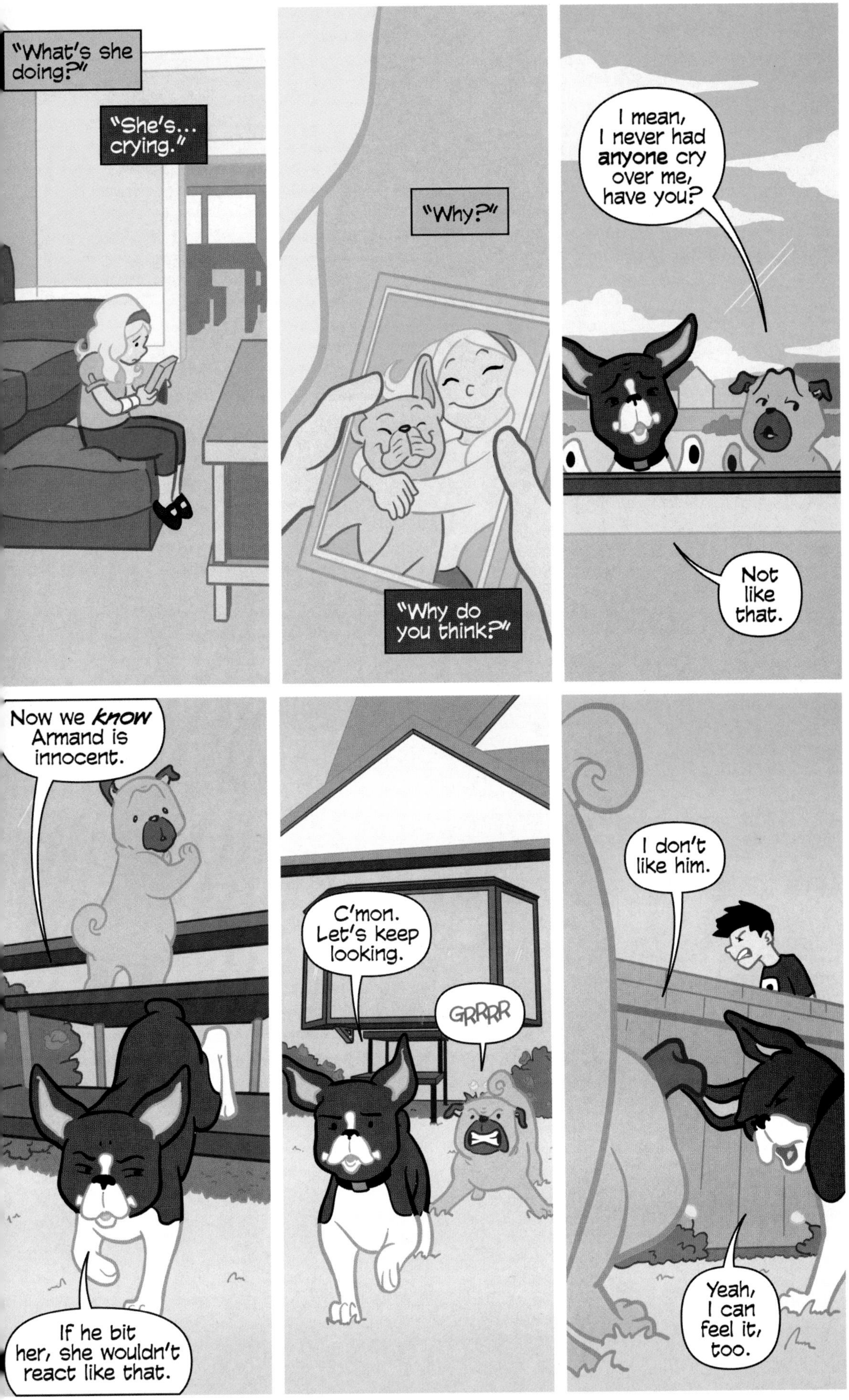
"What's she doing?"
"She's... crying."
"Why?"
"Why do you think?"
I mean, I never had **anyone** cry over me, have you?
Not like that.
Now we *know* Armand is innocent.
If he bit her, she wouldn't react like that.
C'mon. Let's keep looking.
GRRRR
I don't like him.
Yeah, I can feel it, too.

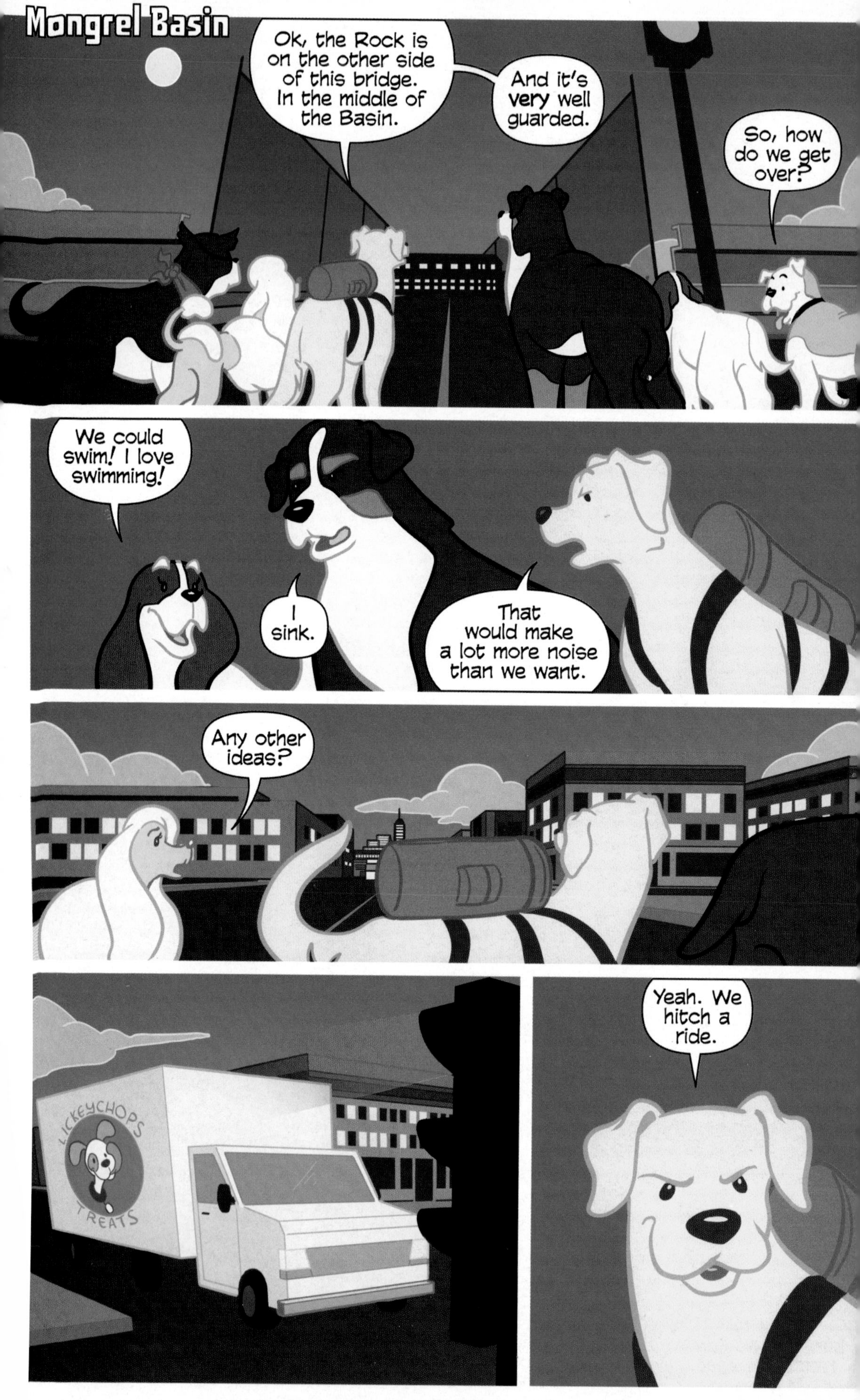
Mongrel Basin
Ok, the Rock is on the other side of this bridge. In the middle of the Basin.
And it's **very** well guarded.
So, how do we get over?
We could swim! I love swimming!
I sink.
That would make a lot more noise than we want.
Any other ideas?
LICKEYCHOPS TREATS
Yeah. We hitch a ride.

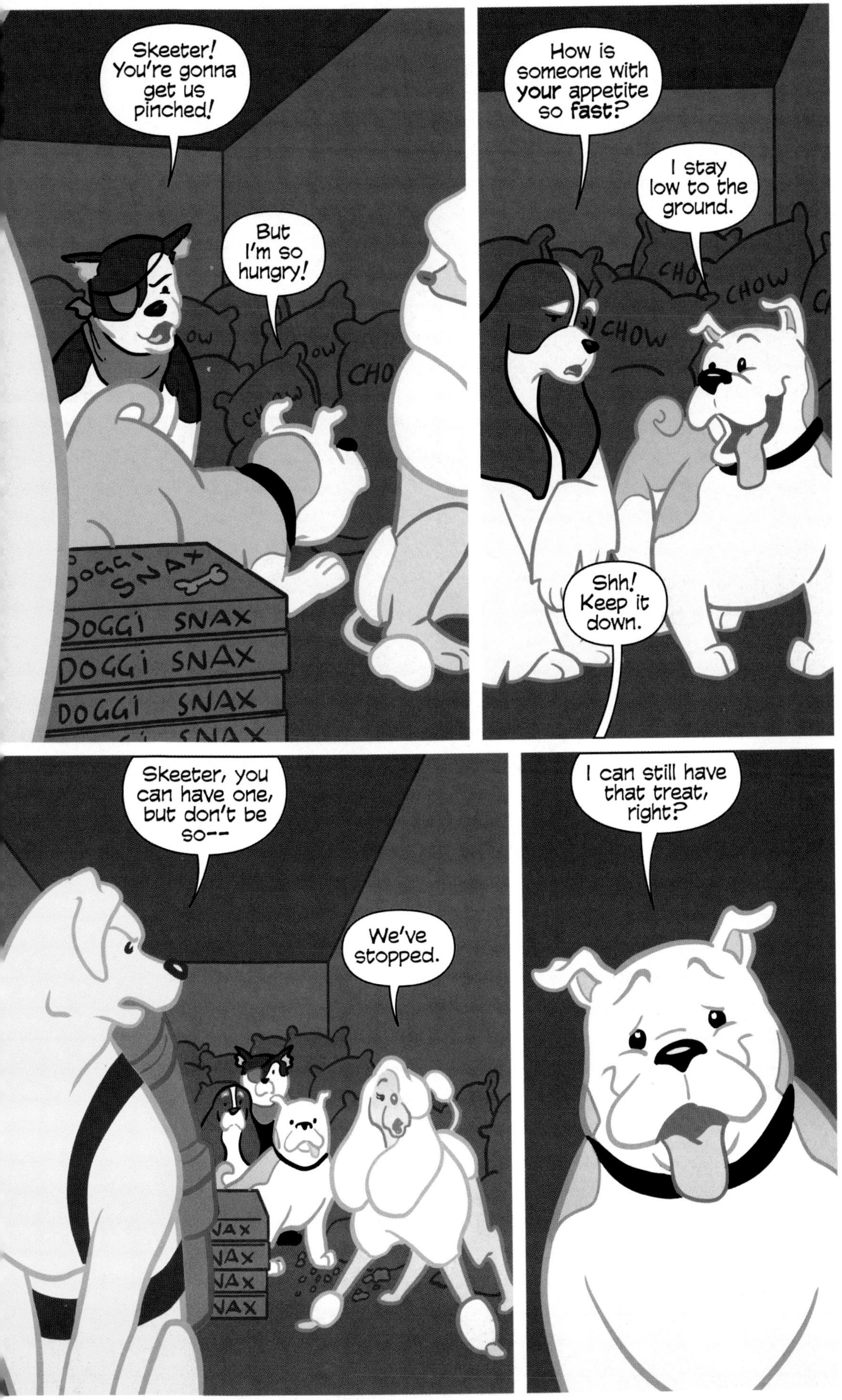

Skeeter! You're gonna get us pinched!
But I'm so hungry!
CHOW
DOGGI SNAX
DOGGI SNAX
DOGGI SNAX
DOGGI SNAX
How is someone with your appetite so fast?
I stay low to the ground.
CHOW
Shh! Keep it down.
Skeeter, you can have one, but don't be so--
We've stopped.
I can still have that treat, right?

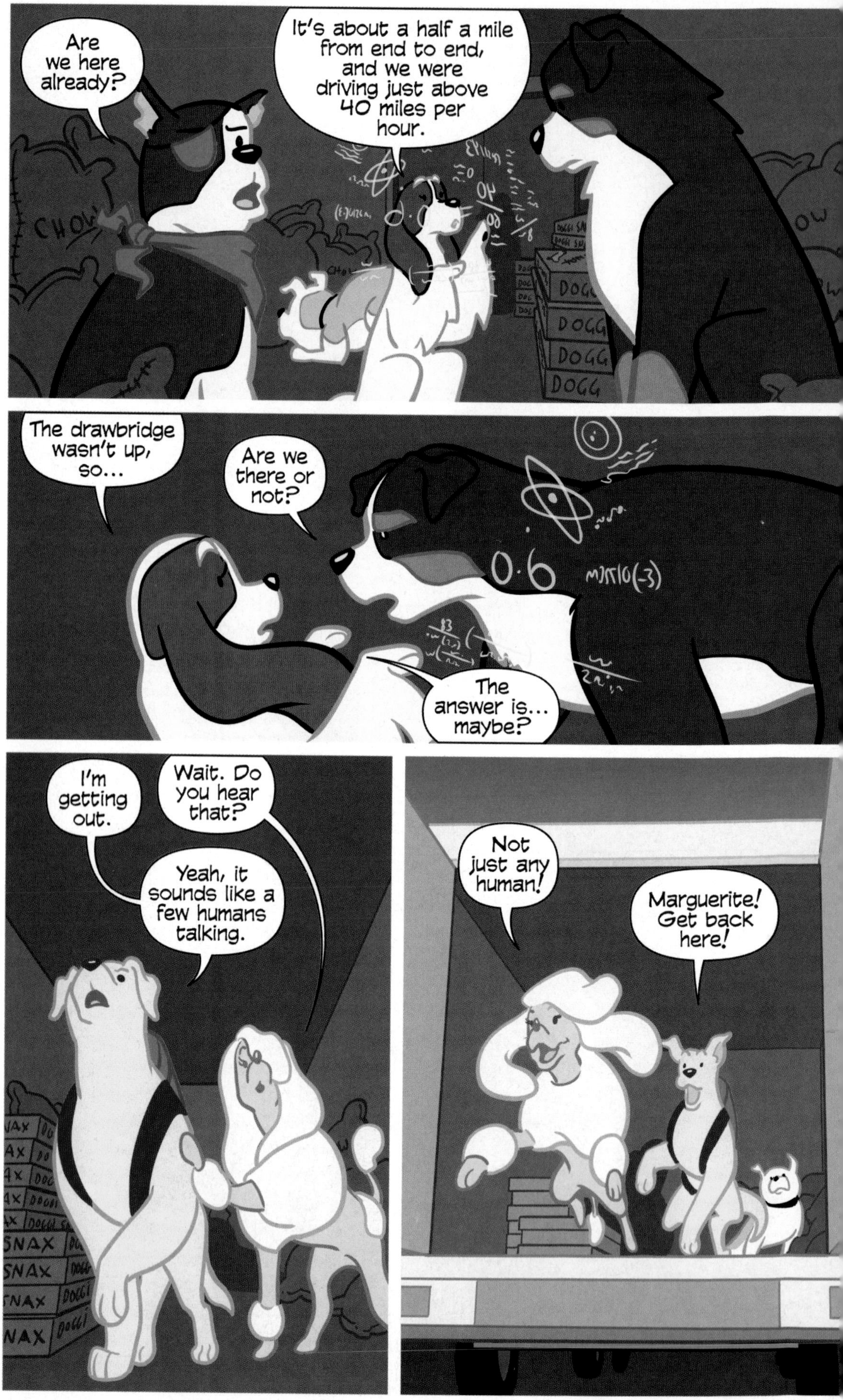
Are we here already?
It's about a half a mile from end to end, and we were driving just above 40 miles per hour.
The drawbridge wasn't up, so...
Are we there or not?
The answer is... maybe?
I'm getting out.
Wait. Do you hear that?
Yeah, it sounds like a few humans talking.
Not just any human!
Marguerite! Get back here!

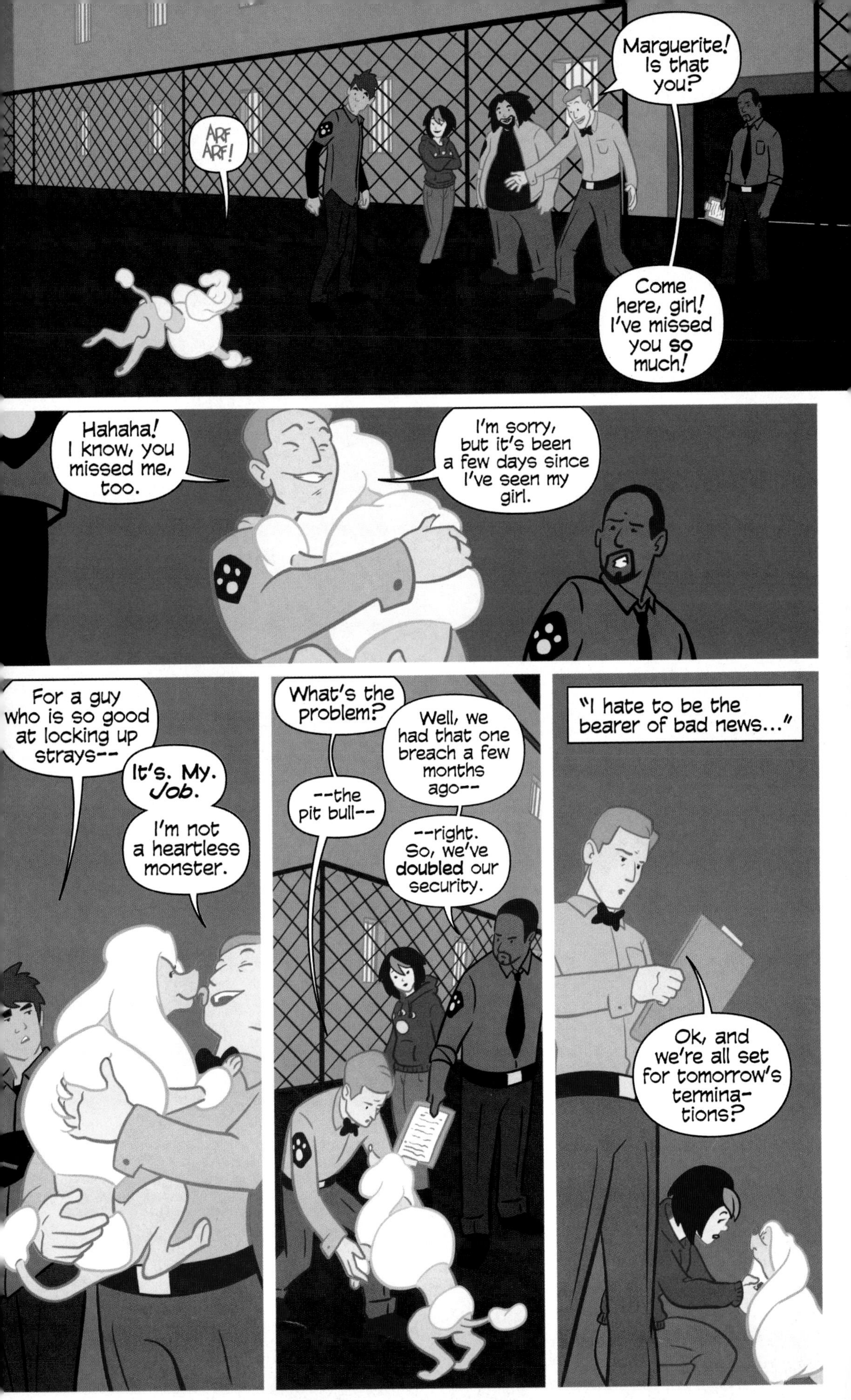
ARF ARF!
Marguerite! Is that you?
Come here, girl! I've missed you so much!
Hahaha! I know, you missed me, too.
I'm sorry, but it's been a few days since I've seen my girl.
For a guy who is so good at locking up strays--
It's. My. Job.
I'm not a heartless monster.
What's the problem?
Well, we had that one breach a few months ago--
--the pit bull--
--right. So, we've doubled our security.
"I hate to be the bearer of bad news..."
Ok, and we're all set for tomorrow's termina-tions?

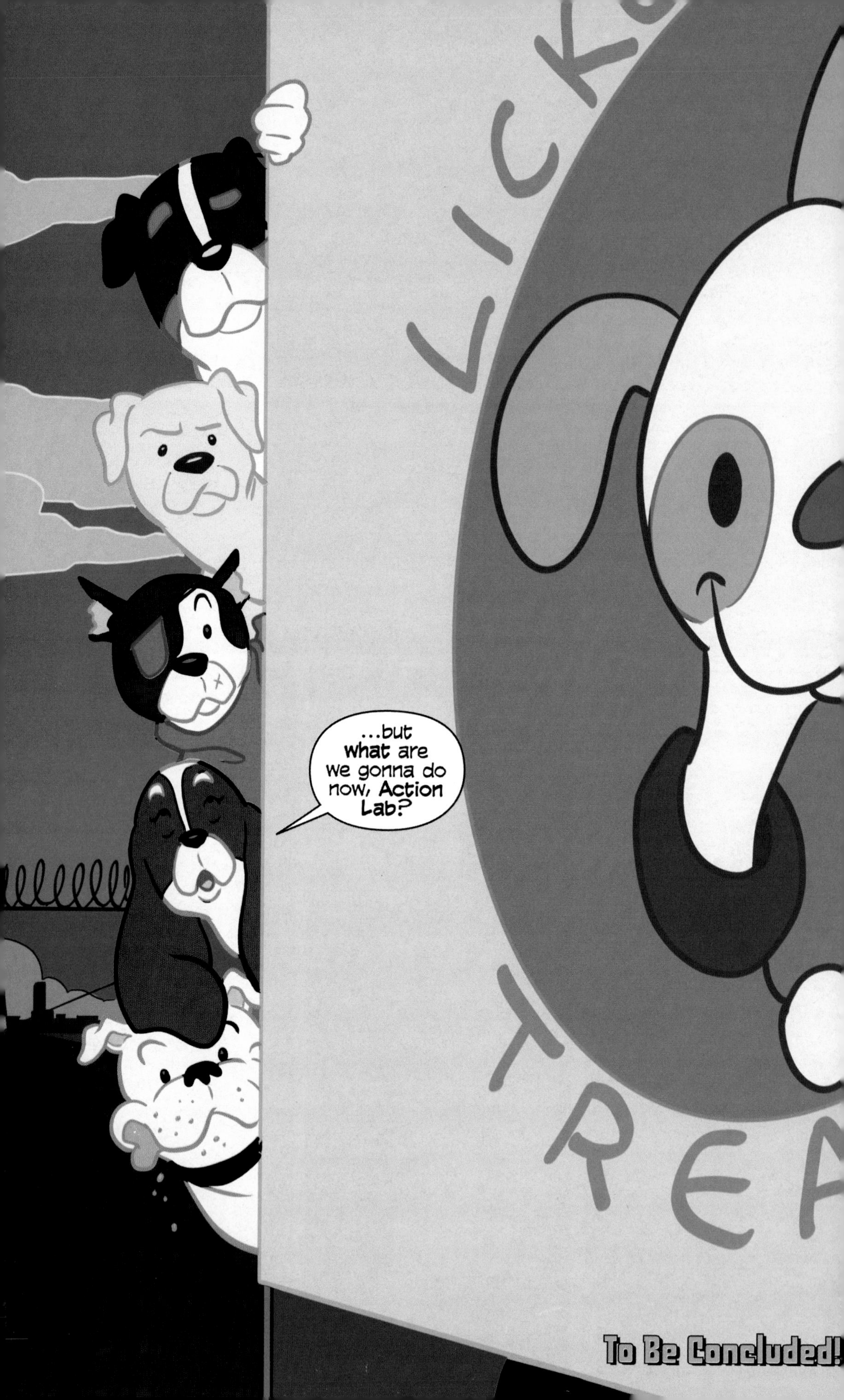
...but what are we gonna do now, Action Lab?
LICK
TREA
To Be Concluded!

In The DOGHOUSE
BY MITZI BOLAÑOS

Greetings from the Doghouse! I write to you from the StubbyDog headquarters, where our volunteers help change the negative stereotypes that surround pit bulls. Here is where you'll find answers to common questions on all things dog! If you have other questions, you can email mitzibolanos@stubbydog.org.

What is spaying and neutering?

These are simple medical procedures done by a veterinarian. Spaying is a procedure for a female dog that will save her from getting pregnant, and neutering is a procedure for a male dog that will make sure he won't get another dog pregnant.

Why does it matter?

Because spaying and neutering saves lives! There are simply too many dogs in our shelters, and unfortunately, only about half of them find families to go home to. Because there aren't enough homes for the other half of the dogs, these dogs are often killed. But don't worry - there's a solution to this problem! As we spay and neuter more dogs, less dogs will enter our shelters, which means that more dogs will have a chance at a loving home. Also, studies show that most dog bite incidents involve unneutered males, so we can help curb dog bites by neutering as well.

Will it hurt my dog?

A veterinarian will perform the procedure on your dog while he's asleep and he won't feel a thing. After the surgery, make sure you give your dog any medicine that the veterinarian prescribes and make sure your dog has a clean, quiet place indoors to rest and recover for at least two weeks.

Will my dog change?

Spaying and neutering can help with many behavioral problems, such as a male dog's urge to escape and roam. However, your dog's personality, all those things that make him special, won't change because that depends on his genes and the environment he lives in, not on whether he can reproduce.

Will my dog get fat?

Spaying and neutering does not affect your dog's weight. Make sure your dog gets plenty of exercise and the right portions of healthy, nutritious food and you won't have to worry about his weight.

Will my dog get sick?

To the contrary! Spaying and neutering can prevent many serious health issues in the future, such as certain forms of cancer. Your dog will live a longer, healthier, and happier life!

Is it expensive?

Just about every community now has an easily accessible low-cost option for spaying and neutering. Check with your local shelter and rescue groups to see what kinds of vouchers they offer. Many groups will sponsor the cost of spay and neuter for families, the elderly, and others. Check online for special deals in your area or contact StubbyDog for help. Remember, the cost of caring for puppies, or potential future health issues, far outweighs the cost of a spay or neuter.

But I love puppies! Can't we have just one litter?

Puppies are awesome! Who doesn't love puppies? Become a volunteer at your local shelter where you'll be able to visit and play with puppies without having to worry about any of the hard work or costs involved in raising them. Keep in mind that even if you find homes for all of your dog's puppies, there's no guarantee that those puppies won't someday end up at a shelter competing for a home with so many other homeless dogs.

Do the responsible thing and prevent that from happening by spaying and neutering!

StubbyDog™
Rediscover the pit bull.

For more information, visit StubbyDog.org!

Thanks, Mitzi! We can't thank you and the great folks at Stubby Dog for all your help!

As you know, we're looking forward to meeting your "action Labs" but while we do, I wanted to introduce you to two special dogs in my life. First up, Kirby:

Kirby is a pitbull and the goofiest dog I ever met. We adopted him from a rescue/no-kill shelter on Staten Island, NY after he was abandoned and found in Snug Harbor, and he has been my best buddy ever since. Kirby is nine years old now, but you would never know it. He still runs fast, jumps up and down...he acts like an over-grown puppy! He has allergies, however, and it makes his skin break out. Luckily, he has the best veterinarian in the world (hi, Dr. Greg Roccaro!).

This next little girl is very special to me and you might recognize her from th[e] issue:

Kasey was a blind American cocke[r] spaniel. Yes, I said "was." Kasey wen[t] to Dog Heaven (or, crossed the Rai[n-]bow Bridge) a few years ago, and n[o] a day goes by where I don't thin[k] about her. She was the BEST dog I hav[e] ever owned, and although I miss her, [I] am so thankful to have had the time w[e] spent together. I have this jacket th[at] she used to curl up in, whenever we'[d] go on long drives, and whenever I se[e] that jacket, I think of my little gir[l.] Because I miss her so much, I put her o[n] the team...so she will always be aroun[d] for me.

Next time, Scott will introduce you t[o] his dogs!

-Vito

NEXT ISSUE: How will Percy and the Action Lab League get out of this one? Double-crossed by Marguerite and Armand has only hours left to go! Be here in 60 days for the conclusion of "Who Let the Dogs Out?"

Email us at PercyTheDogOfWonder@gmail.com!

PrinceVess

RAVEN: THE PIRATE PRINCESS

THE SECOND VOLUME OF JEREMY WHITLEY'S GROUNDBREAKING SERIES... COLLECTED!

ON SALE NOW!

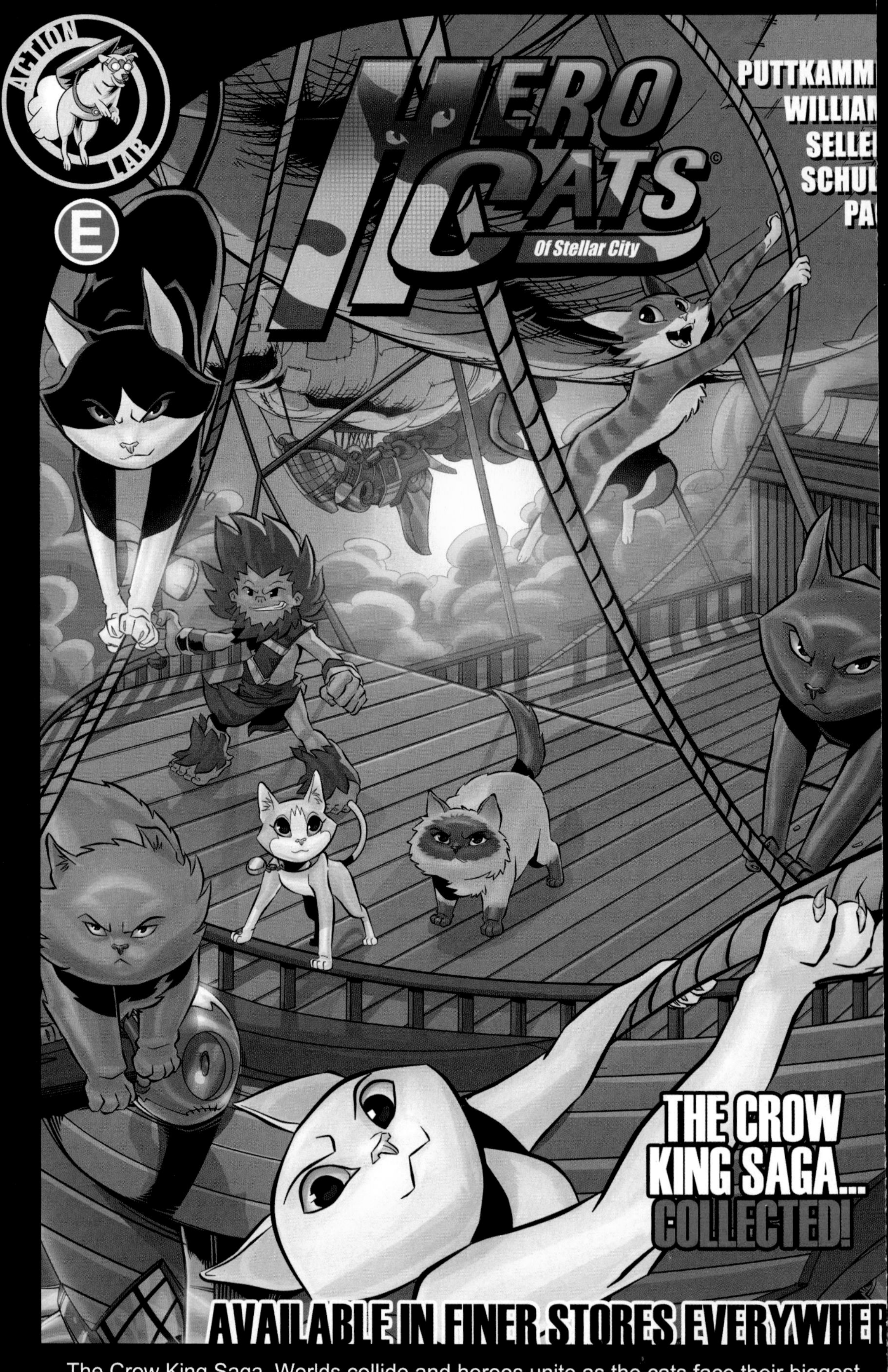
ACTION LAB
E
HERO CATS
Of Stellar City
PUTTKAMM
WILLIAM
SELLE
SCHUL
PA
THE CROW KING SAGA...
COLLECTED!
AVAILABLE IN FINER STORES EVERYWHER

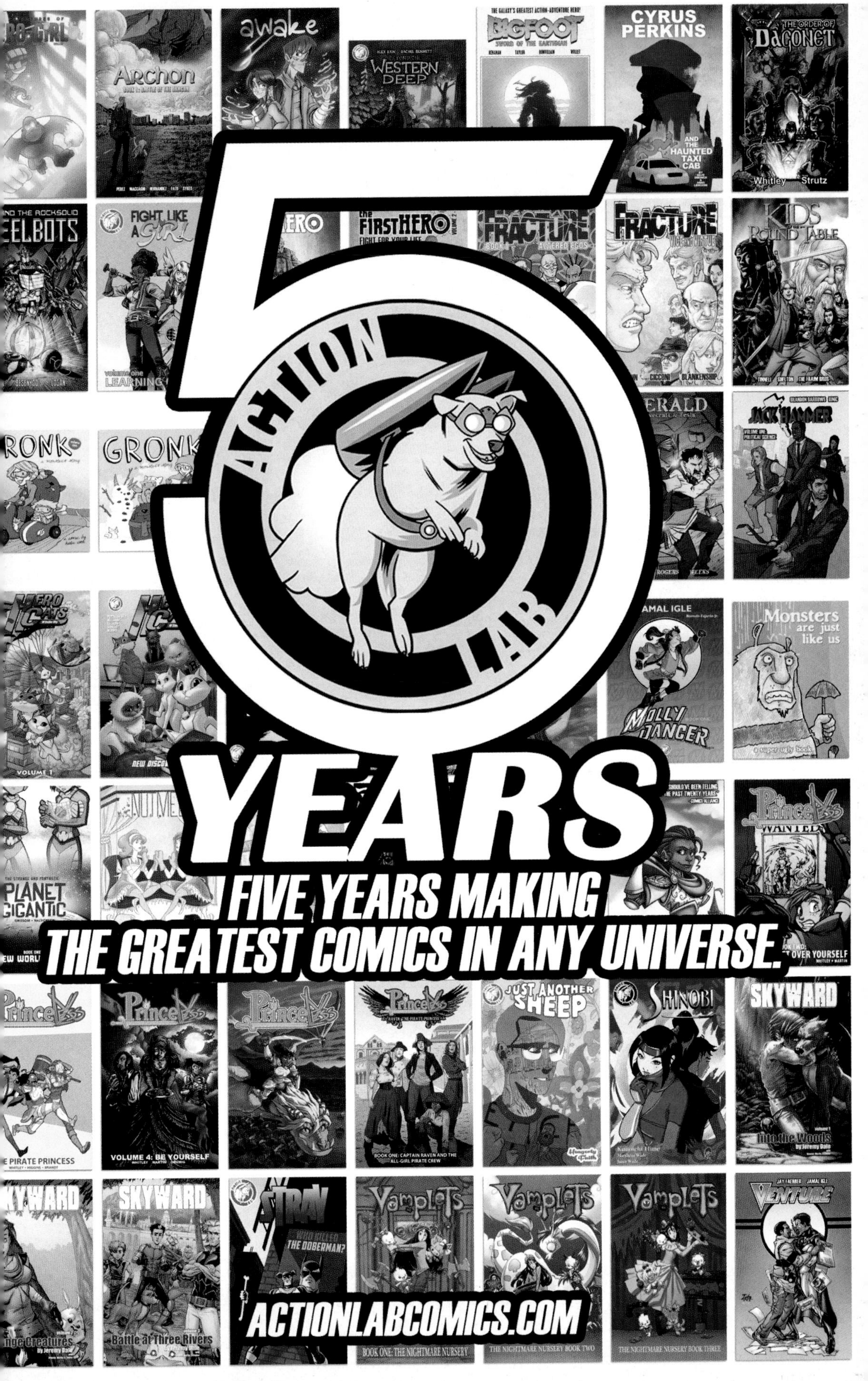

5
ACTION LAB
YEARS
FIVE YEARS MAKING
THE GREATEST COMICS IN ANY UNIVERSE.
ACTIONLABCOMICS.COM

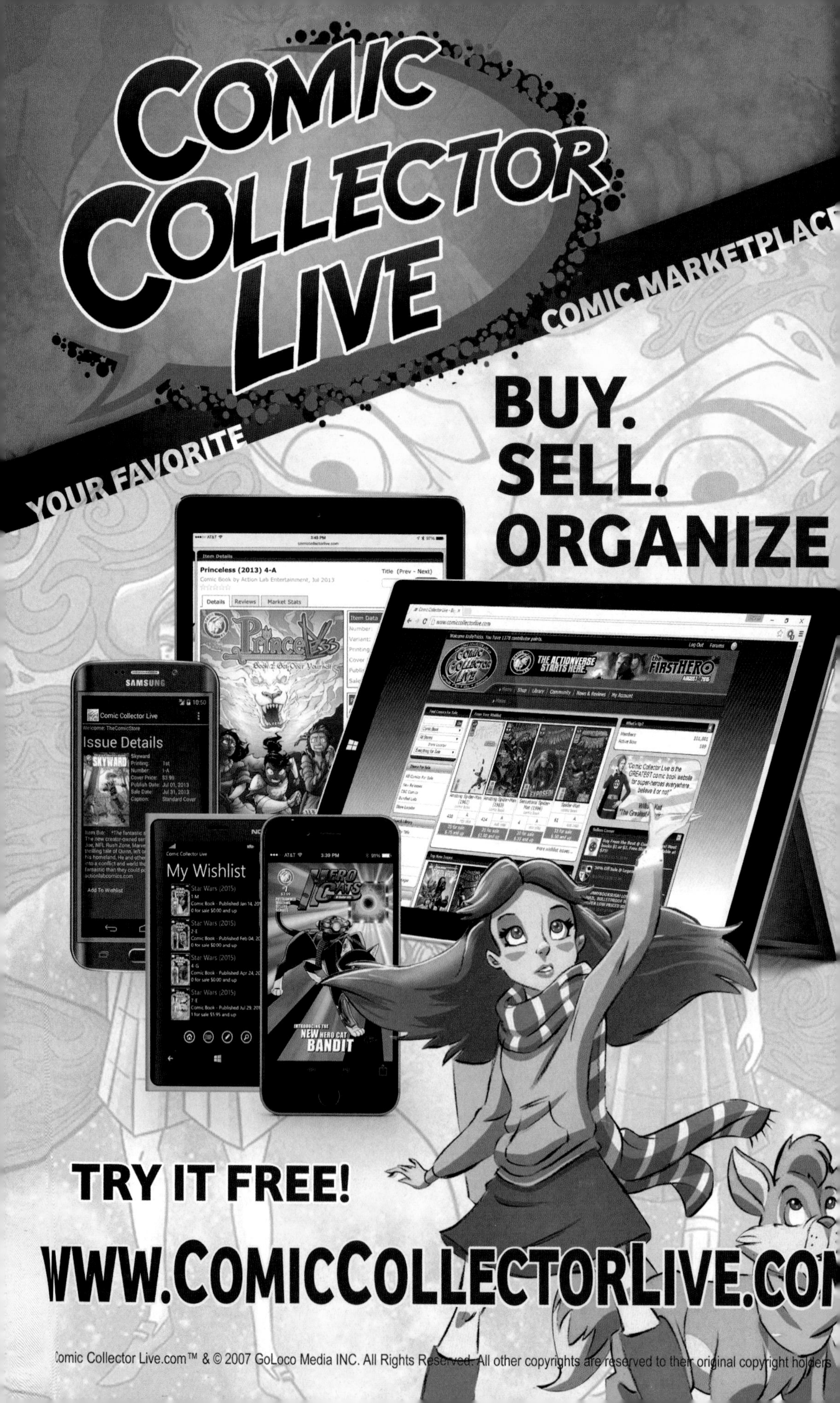
COMIC COLLECTOR LIVE
YOUR FAVORITE COMIC MARKETPLACE
BUY.
SELL.
ORGANIZE
TRY IT FREE!
WWW.COMICCOLLECTORLIVE.COM
Comic Collector Live.com™ & © 2007 GoLoco Media INC. All Rights Reserved. All other copyrights are reserved to their original copyright holders

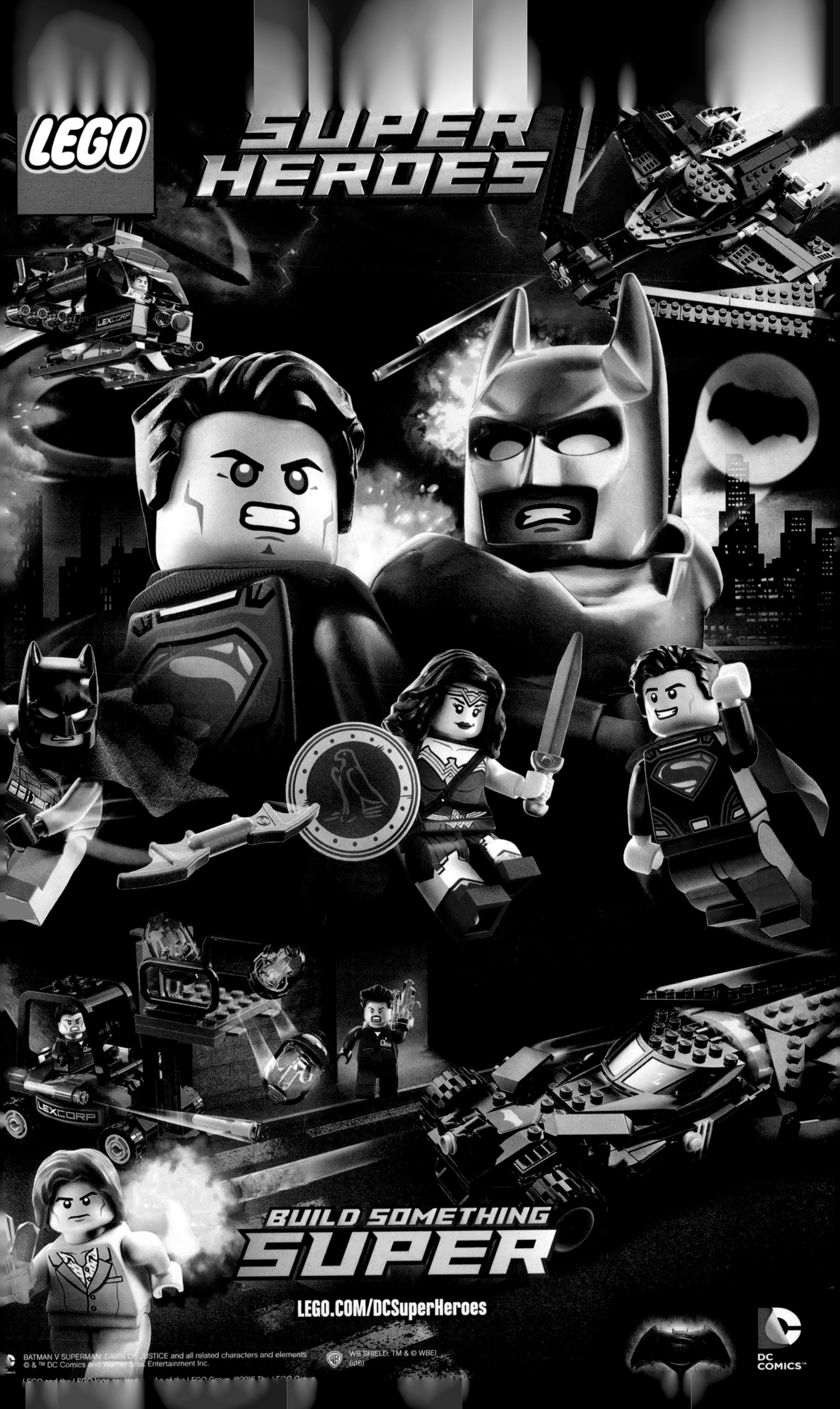

LEGO
SUPER HEROES
LEXCORP
BUILD SOMETHING SUPER
LEGO.COM/DCSuperHeroes
BATMAN V SUPERMAN: DAWN OF JUSTICE and all related characters and elements © & ™ DC Comics and Warner Bros. Entertainment Inc.
WB SHIELD: TM & © WBEI (s16)
DC COMICS

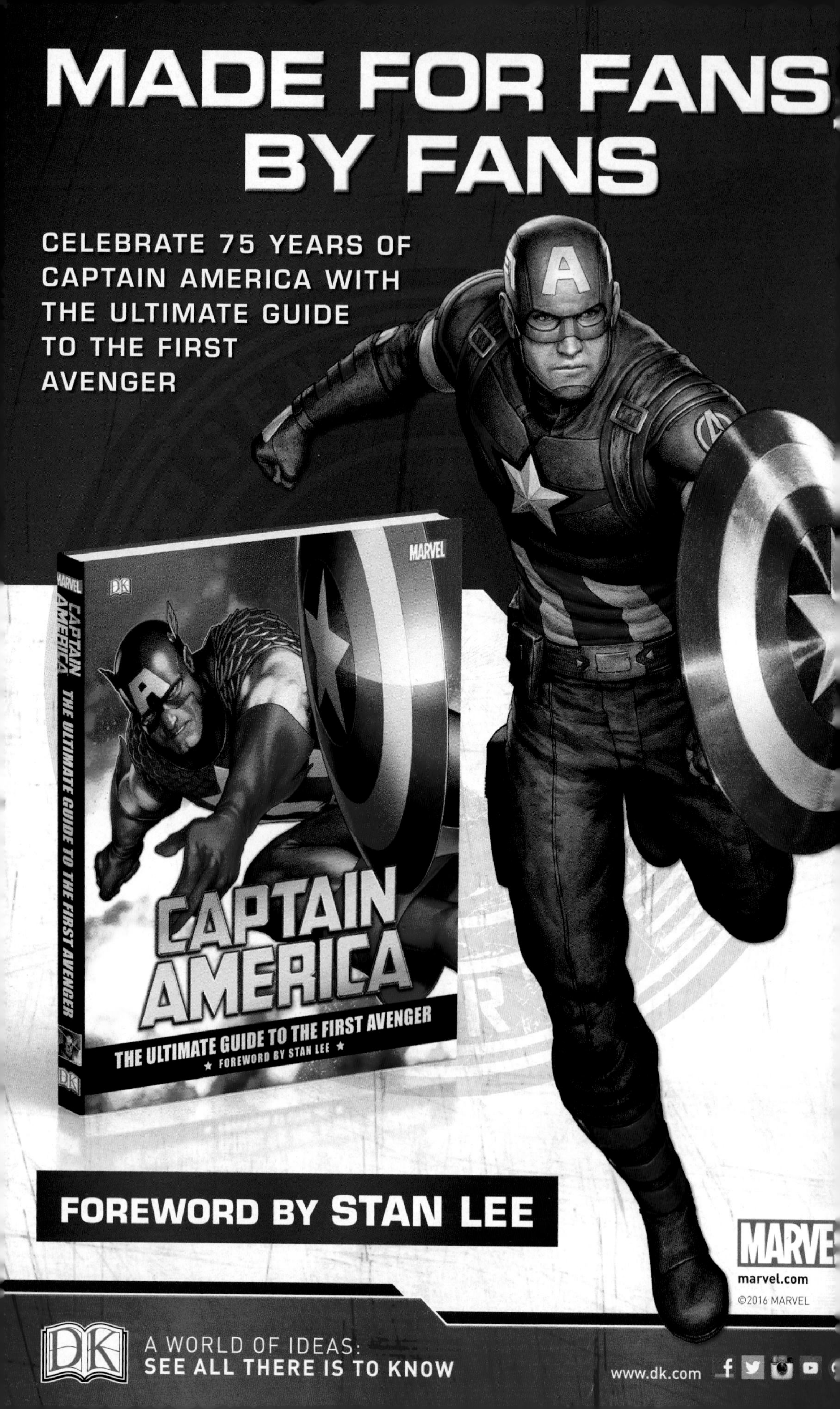
MADE FOR FANS
BY FANS
CELEBRATE 75 YEARS OF CAPTAIN AMERICA WITH THE ULTIMATE GUIDE TO THE FIRST AVENGER
MARVEL
DK
CAPTAIN AMERICA
THE ULTIMATE GUIDE TO THE FIRST AVENGER
★ FOREWORD BY STAN LEE ★
FOREWORD BY STAN LEE
MARVEL
marvel.com
©2016 MARVEL
DK
A WORLD OF IDEAS:
SEE ALL THERE IS TO KNOW
www.dk.com

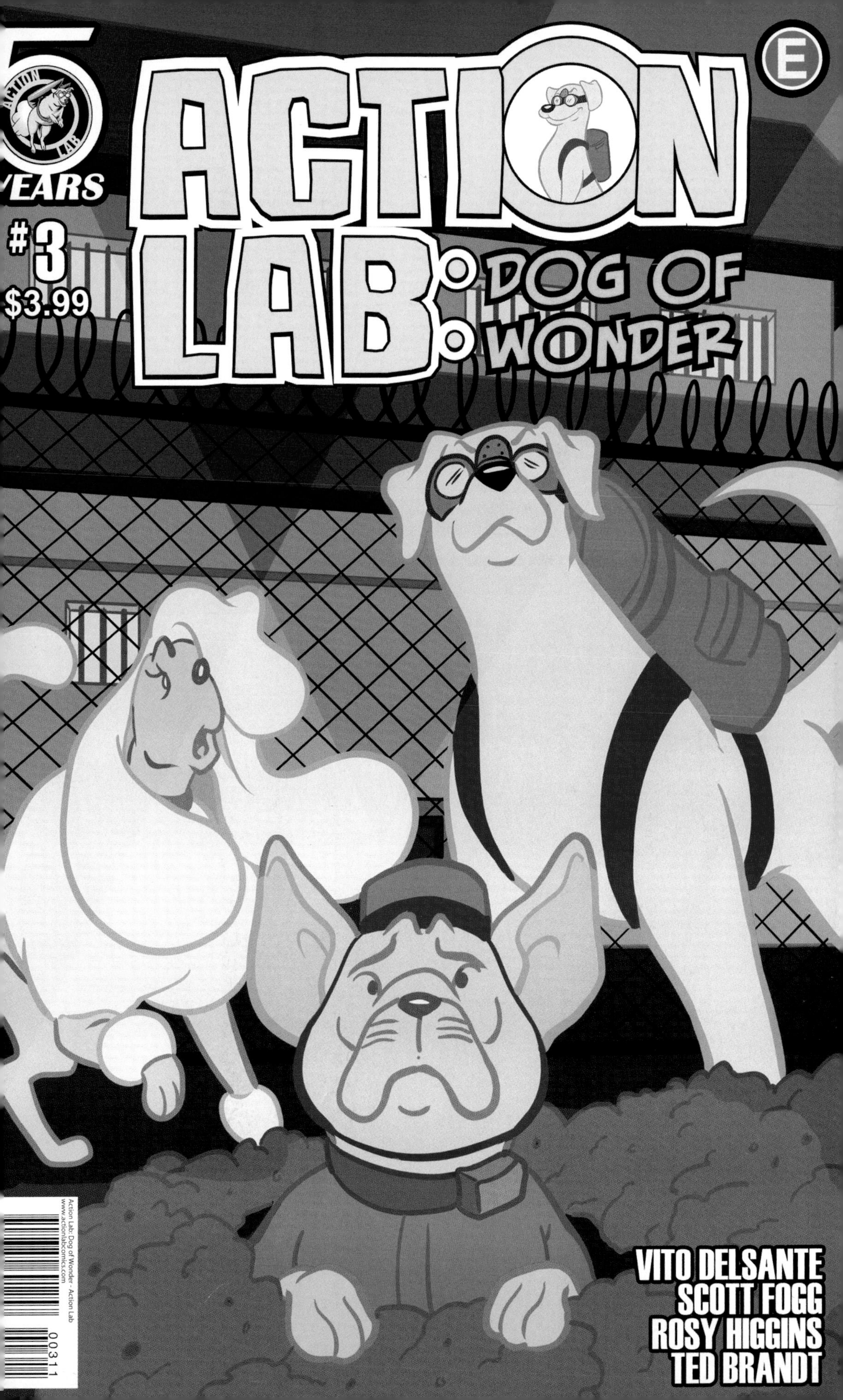
5 YEARS
#3
$3.99
ACTION LAB: DOG OF WONDER
E
VITO DELSANTE
SCOTT FOGG
ROSY HIGGINS
TED BRANDT

COMIC COLLECTOR LIVE

COMIC MARKETPLACE

YOUR FAVORITE

BUY.
SELL.
ORGANIZE.

TRY IT FREE!

WWW.COMICCOLLECTORLIVE.COM

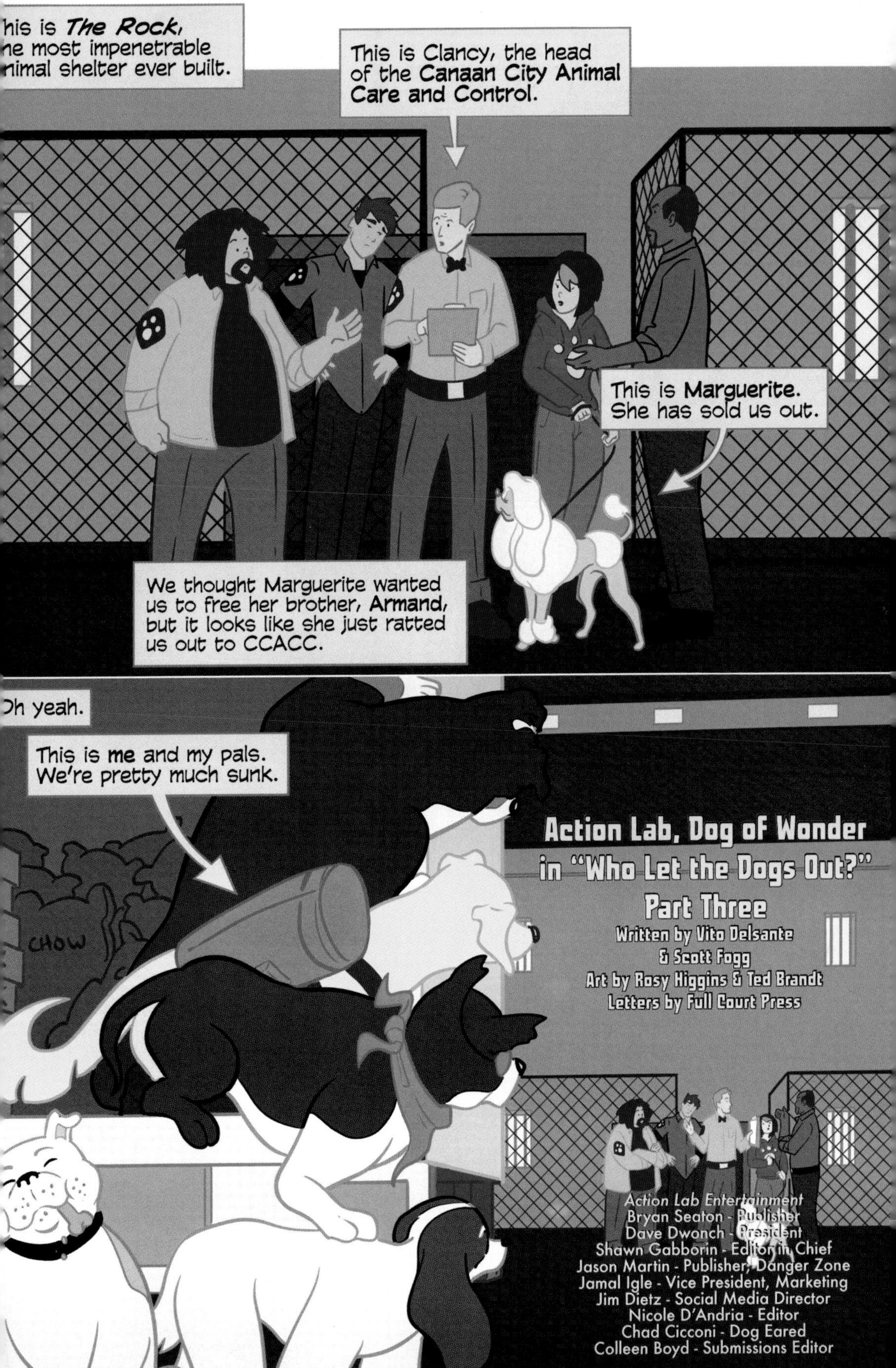

his is *The Rock*,
he most impenetrable
nimal shelter ever built.
This is Clancy, the head of the **Canaan City Animal Care and Control.**
This is **Marguerite.** She has sold us out.
We thought Marguerite wanted us to free her brother, **Armand,** but it looks like she just ratted us out to CCACC.
Oh yeah.
This is **me** and my pals. We're pretty much sunk.
CHOW
Action Lab, Dog of Wonder
in "Who Let the Dogs Out?"
Part Three
Written by Vito Delsante
& Scott Fogg
Art by Rosy Higgins & Ted Brandt
Letters by Full Court Press
Action Lab Entertainment
Bryan Seaton - Publisher
Dave Dwonch - President
Shawn Gabborin - Editor in Chief
Jason Martin - Publisher, Danger Zone
Jamal Igle - Vice President, Marketing
Jim Dietz - Social Media Director
Nicole D'Andria - Editor
Chad Cicconi - Dog Eared
Colleen Boyd - Submissions Editor

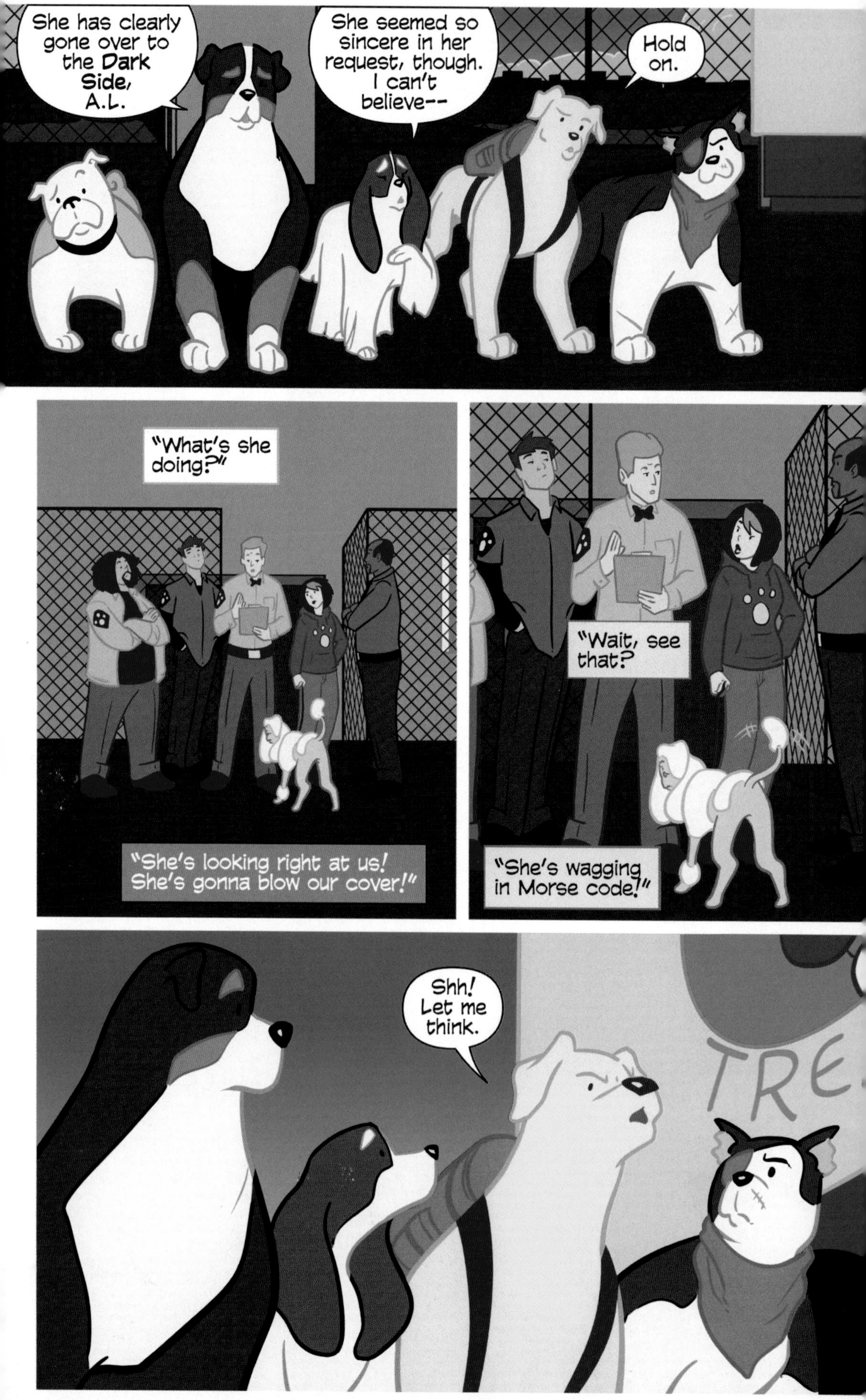
She has clearly gone over to the **Dark Side**, A.L.
She seemed so sincere in her request, though. I can't believe--
Hold on.
"What's she doing?"
"She's looking right at us! She's gonna blow our cover!"
"Wait, see that?
"She's wagging in Morse code!"
Shh! Let me think.
TRE

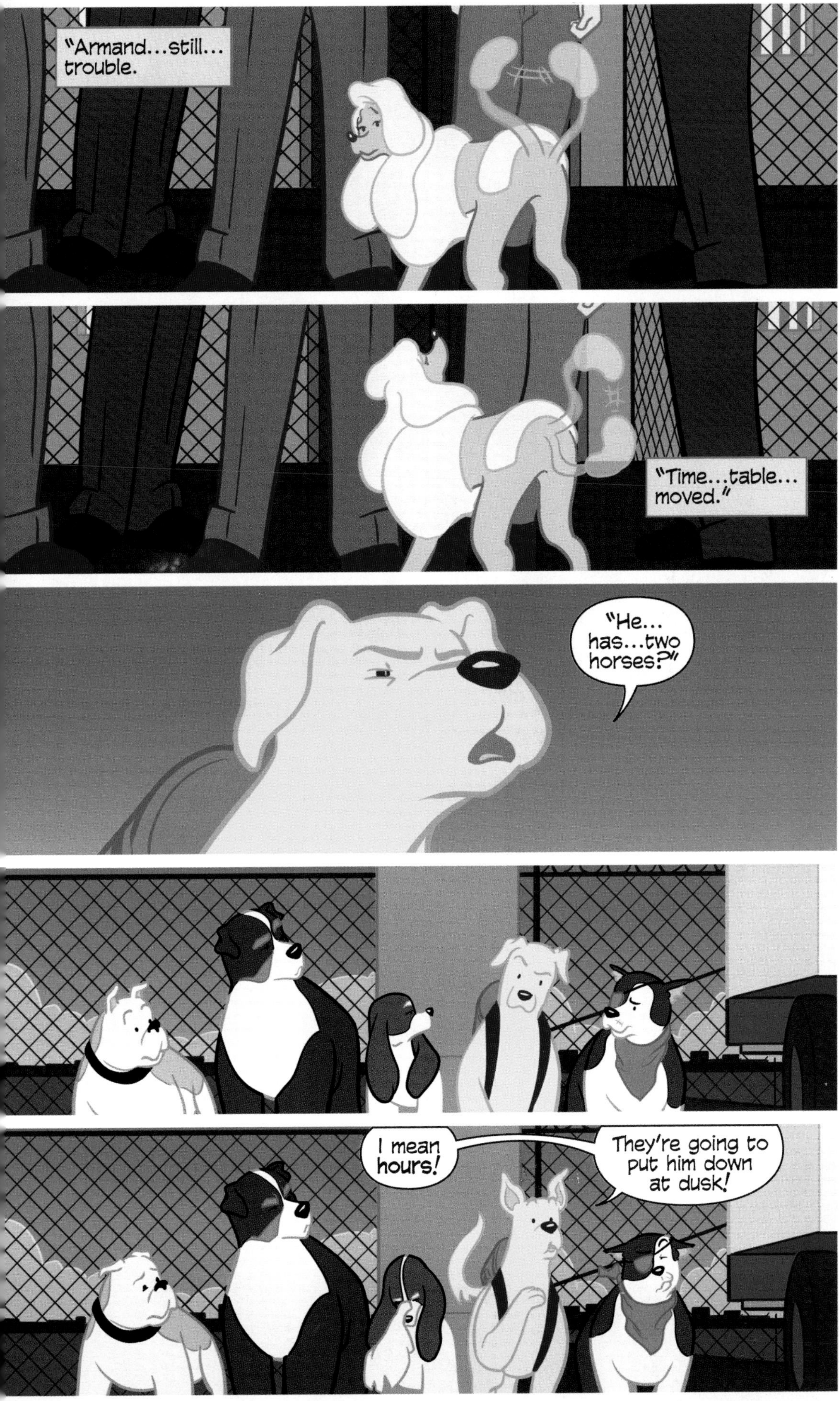
"Armand...still... trouble.
"Time...table... moved."
"He... has...two horses?"
I mean hours!
They're going to put him down at dusk!

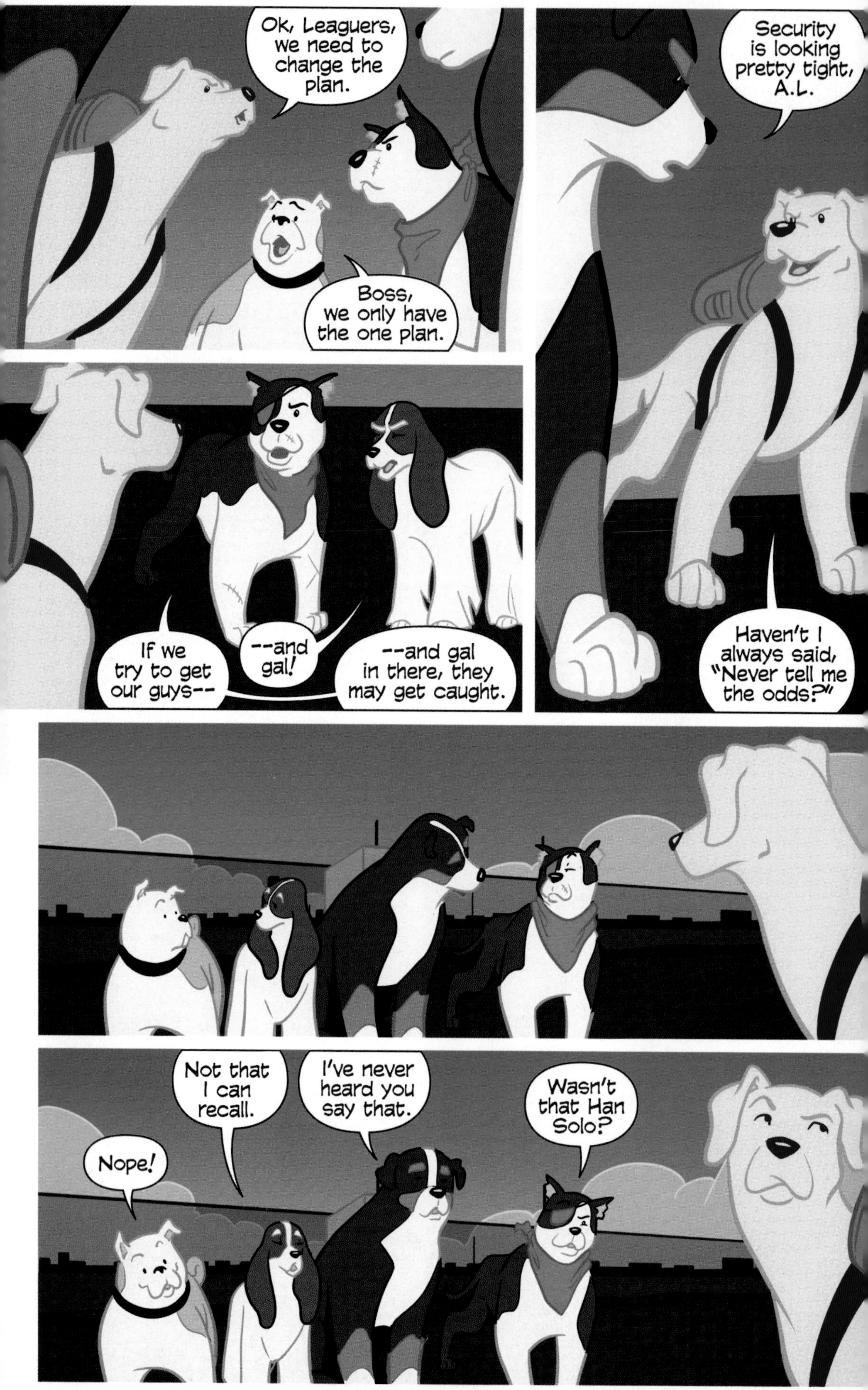
Ok, Leaguers, we need to change the plan.
Boss, we only have the one plan.
Security is looking pretty tight, A.L.
If we try to get our guys--
--and gal!
--and gal in there, they may get caught.
Haven't I always said, "Never tell me the odds?"
Nope!
Not that I can recall.
I've never heard you say that.
Wasn't that Han Solo?

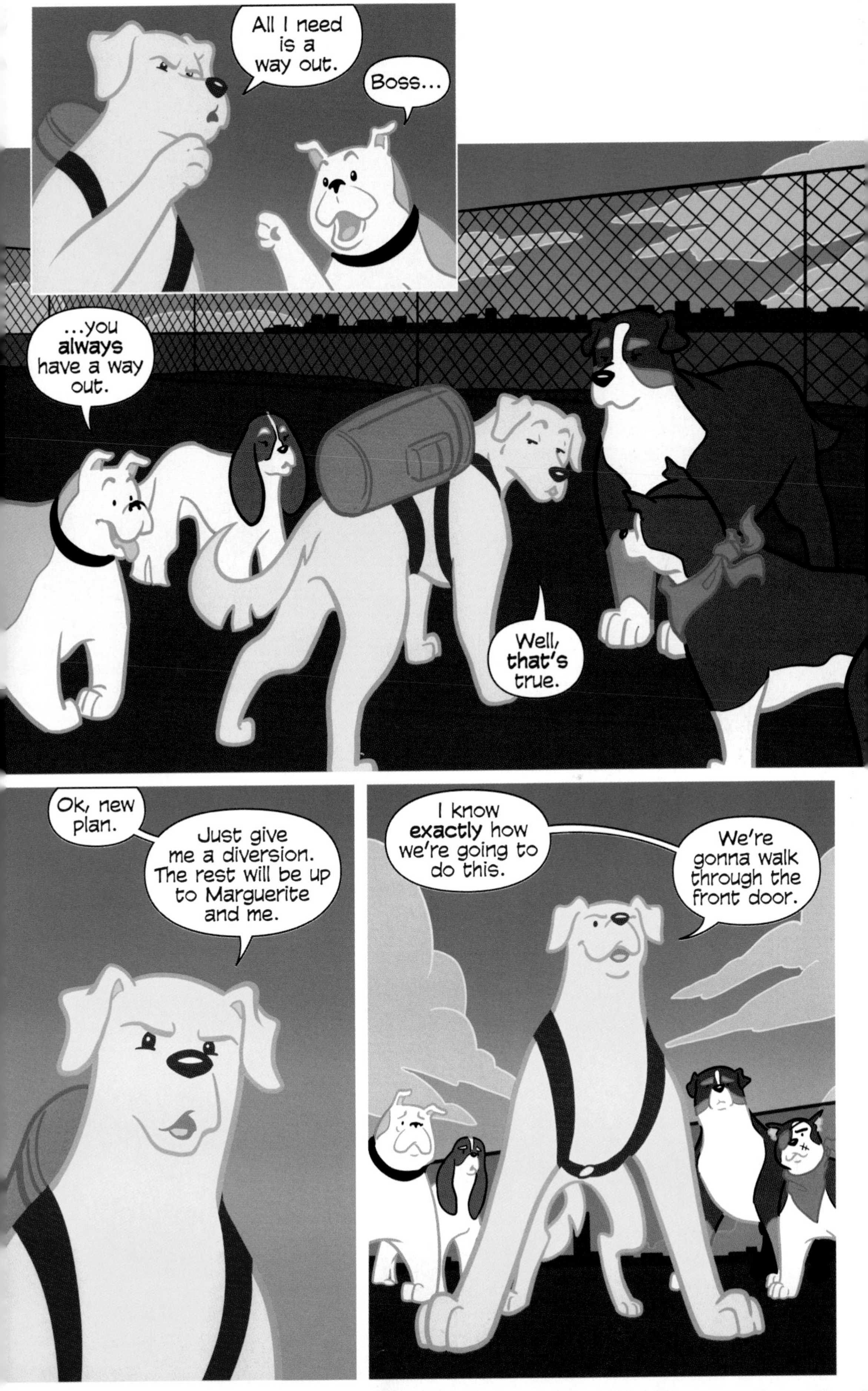

All I need is a way out.
Boss...
...you always have a way out.
Well, that's true.
Ok, new plan.
Just give me a diversion. The rest will be up to Marguerite and me.
I know exactly how we're going to do this.
We're gonna walk through the front door.

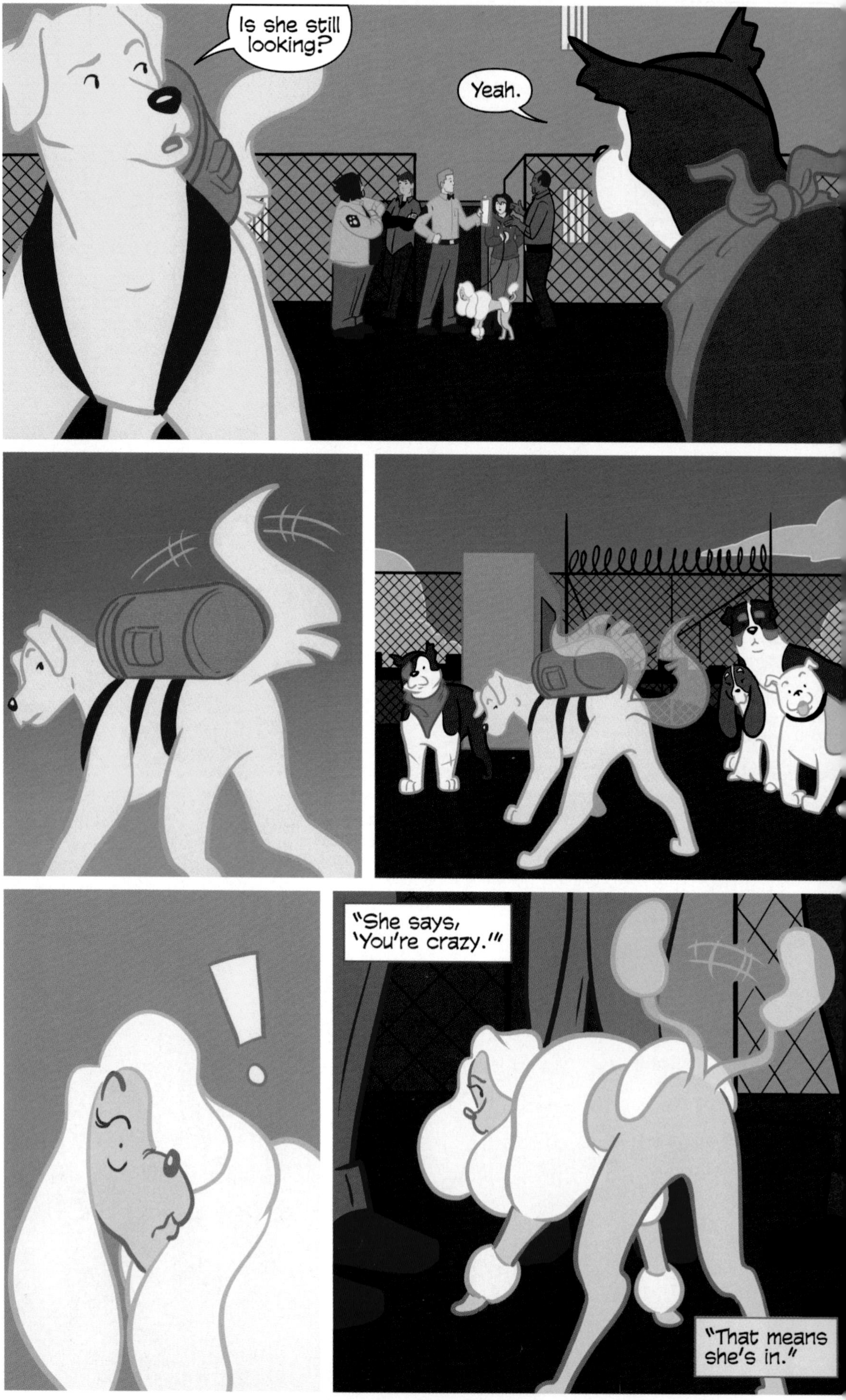

Is she still looking?
Yeah.
"She says, 'You're crazy.'"
"That means she's in."

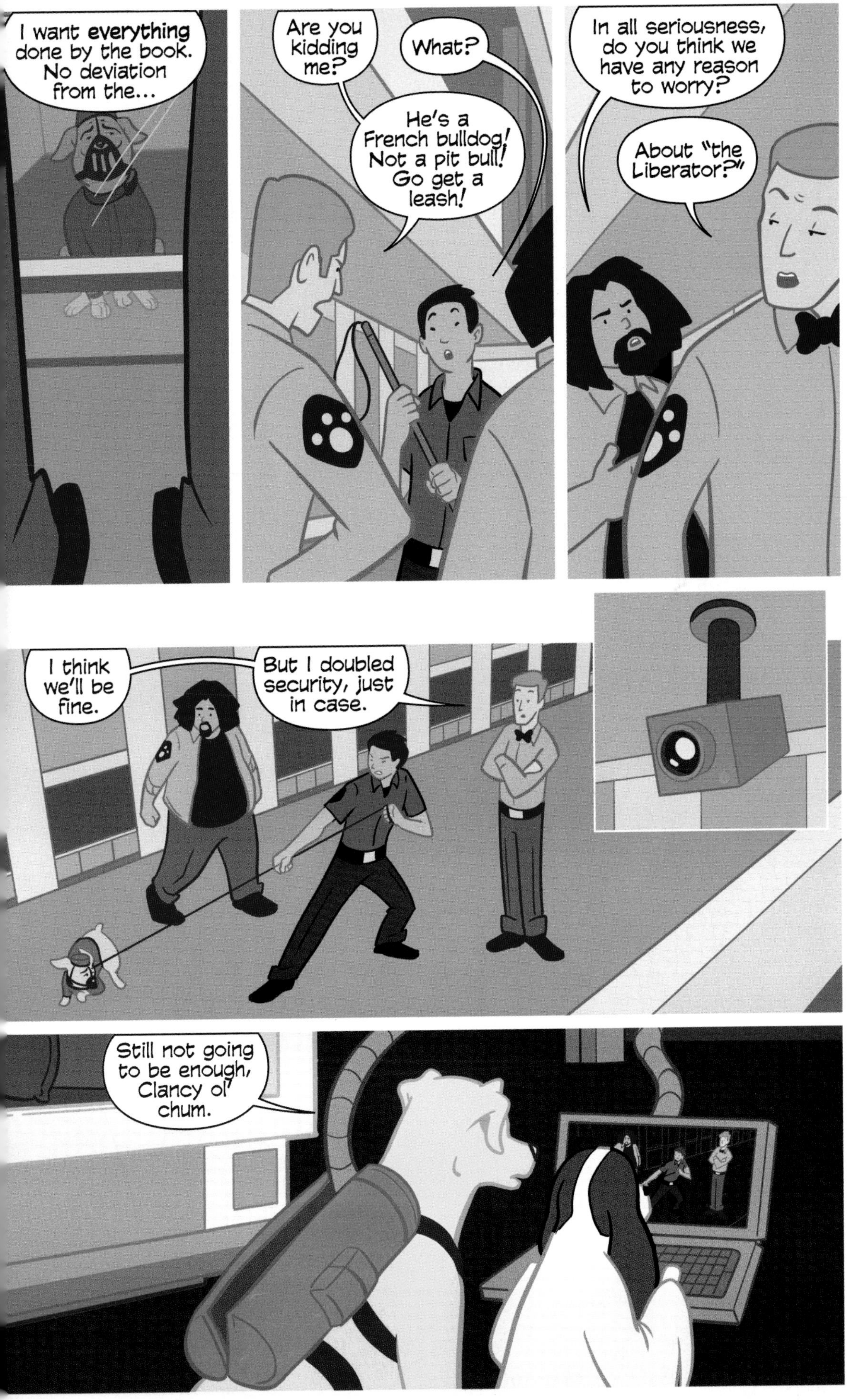
I want **everything** done by the book. No deviation from the...
Are you kidding me?
What?
He's a French bulldog! Not a pit bull! Go get a leash!
In all seriousness, do you think we have any reason to worry?
About "the Liberator?"
I think we'll be fine.
But I doubled security, just in case.
Still not going to be enough, Clancy ol' chum.

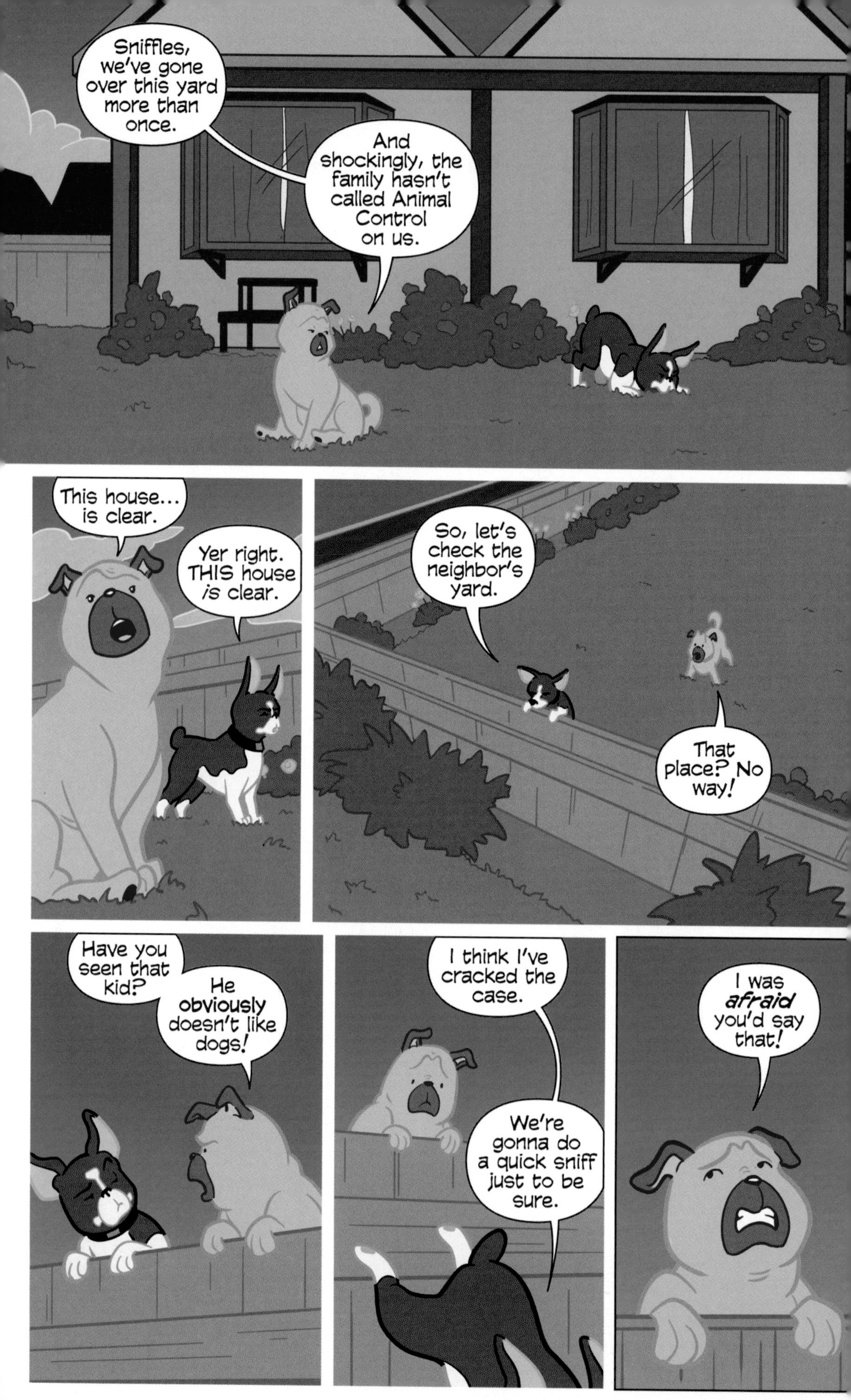

Sniffles, we've gone over this yard more than once.
And shockingly, the family hasn't called Animal Control on us.
This house... is clear.
Yer right. THIS house *is* clear.
So, let's check the neighbor's yard.
That place? No way!
Have you seen that kid?
He obviously doesn't like dogs!
I think I've cracked the case.
We're gonna do a quick sniff just to be sure.
I was ***afraid*** you'd say that!

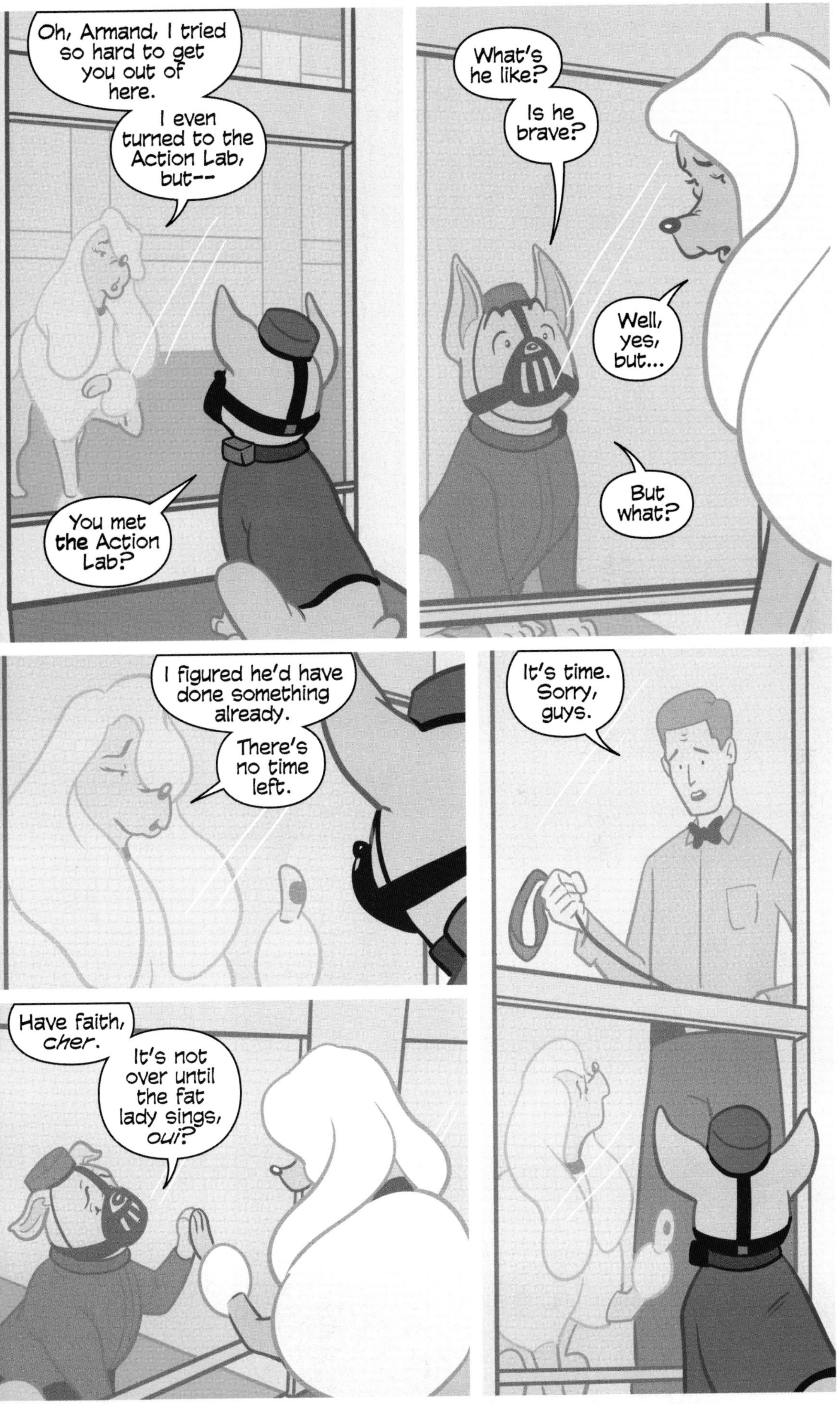
Oh, Armand, I tried so hard to get you out of here.
I even turned to the Action Lab, but--
You met **the** Action Lab?
What's he like?
Is he brave?
Well, yes, but...
But what?
I figured he'd have done something already.
There's no time left.
It's time. Sorry, guys.
Have faith, *cher*.
It's not over until the fat lady sings, *oui*?

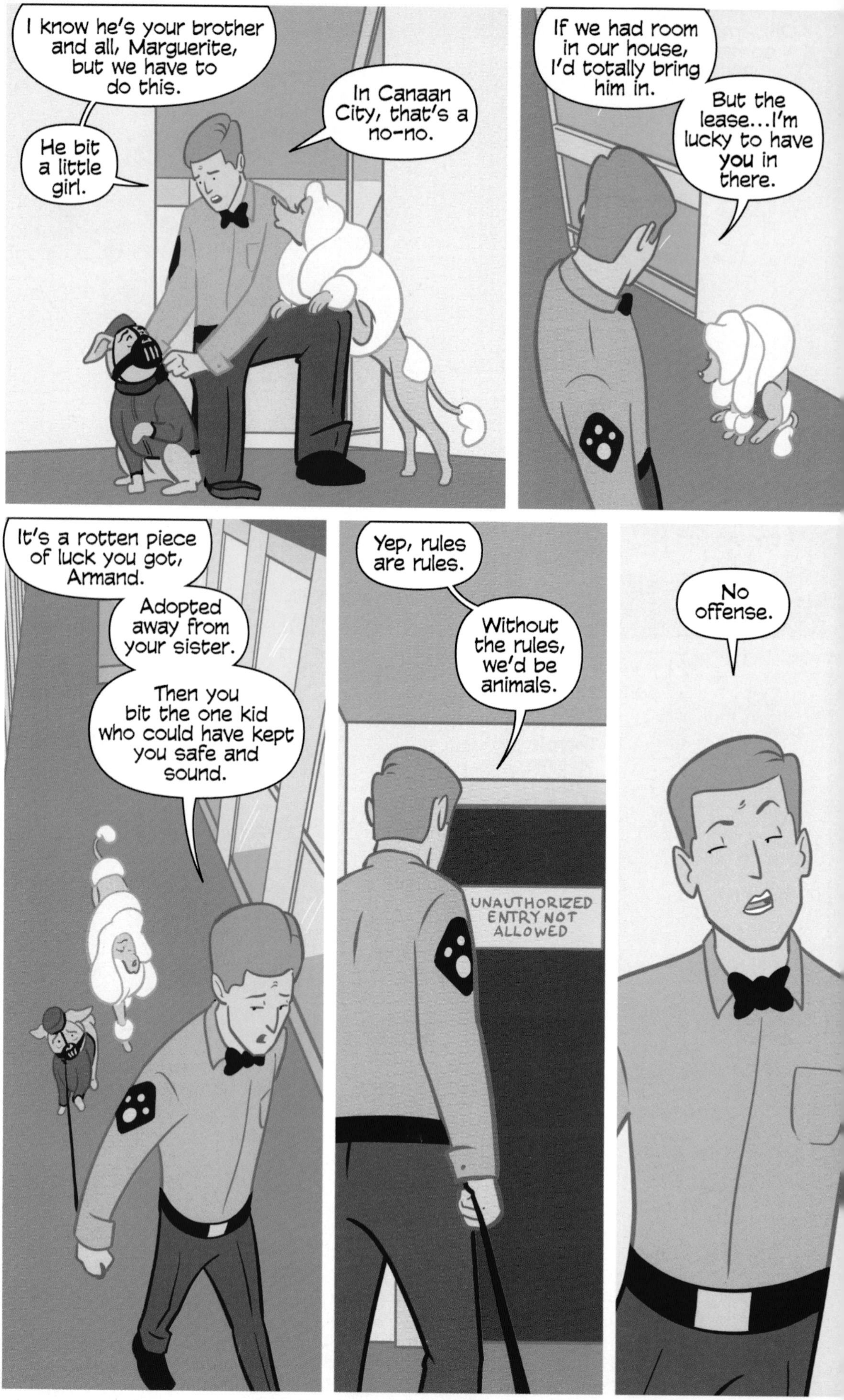
I know he's your brother and all, Marguerite, but we have to do this.
He bit a little girl.
In Canaan City, that's a no-no.
If we had room in our house, I'd totally bring him in.
But the lease...I'm lucky to have you in there.
It's a rotten piece of luck you got, Armand.
Adopted away from your sister.
Then you bit the one kid who could have kept you safe and sound.
Yep, rules are rules.
Without the rules, we'd be animals.
UNAUTHORIZED ENTRY NOT ALLOWED
No offense.

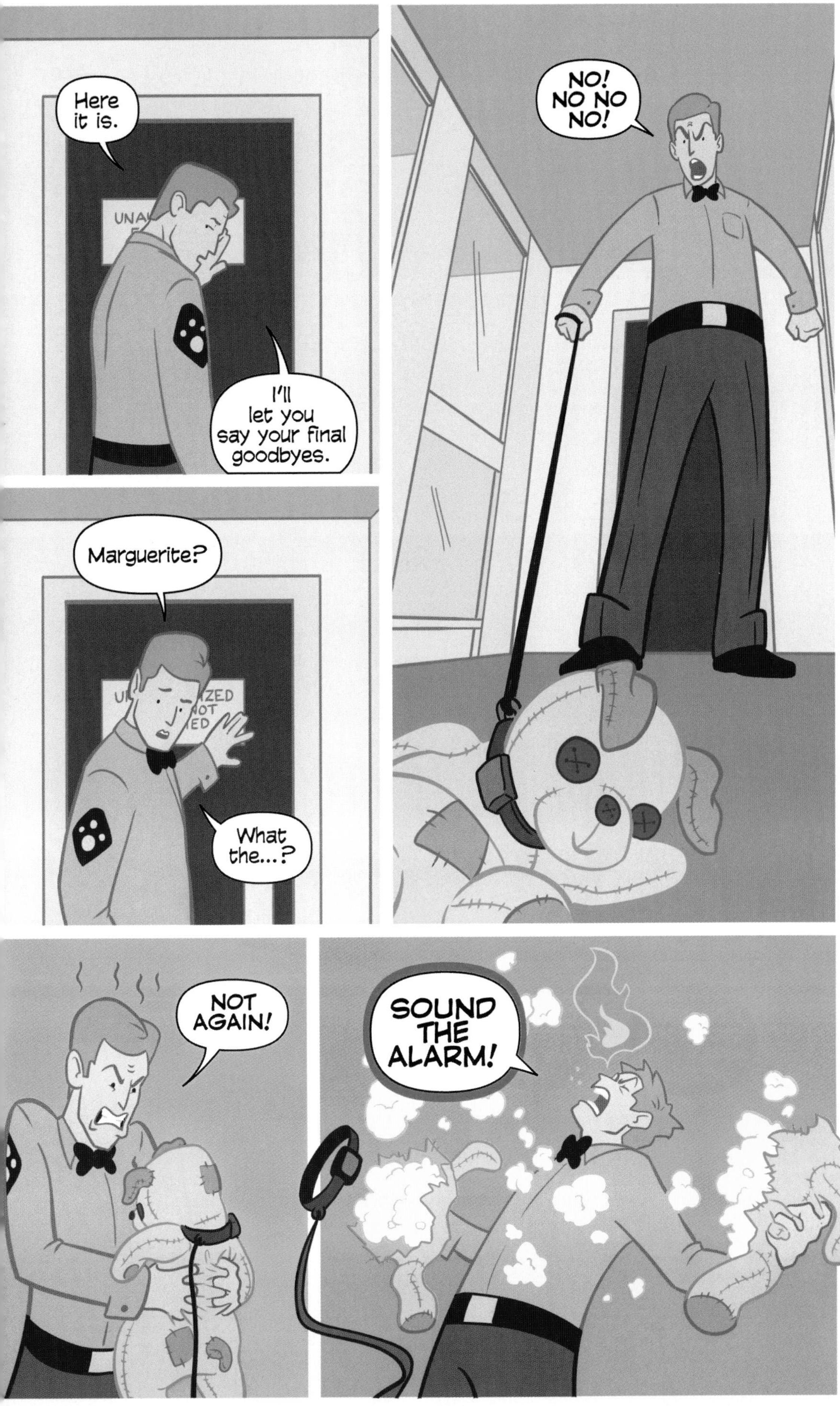
Here it is.
I'll let you say your final goodbyes.
Marguerite?
What the...?
NO! NO NO NO!
NOT AGAIN!
SOUND THE ALARM!

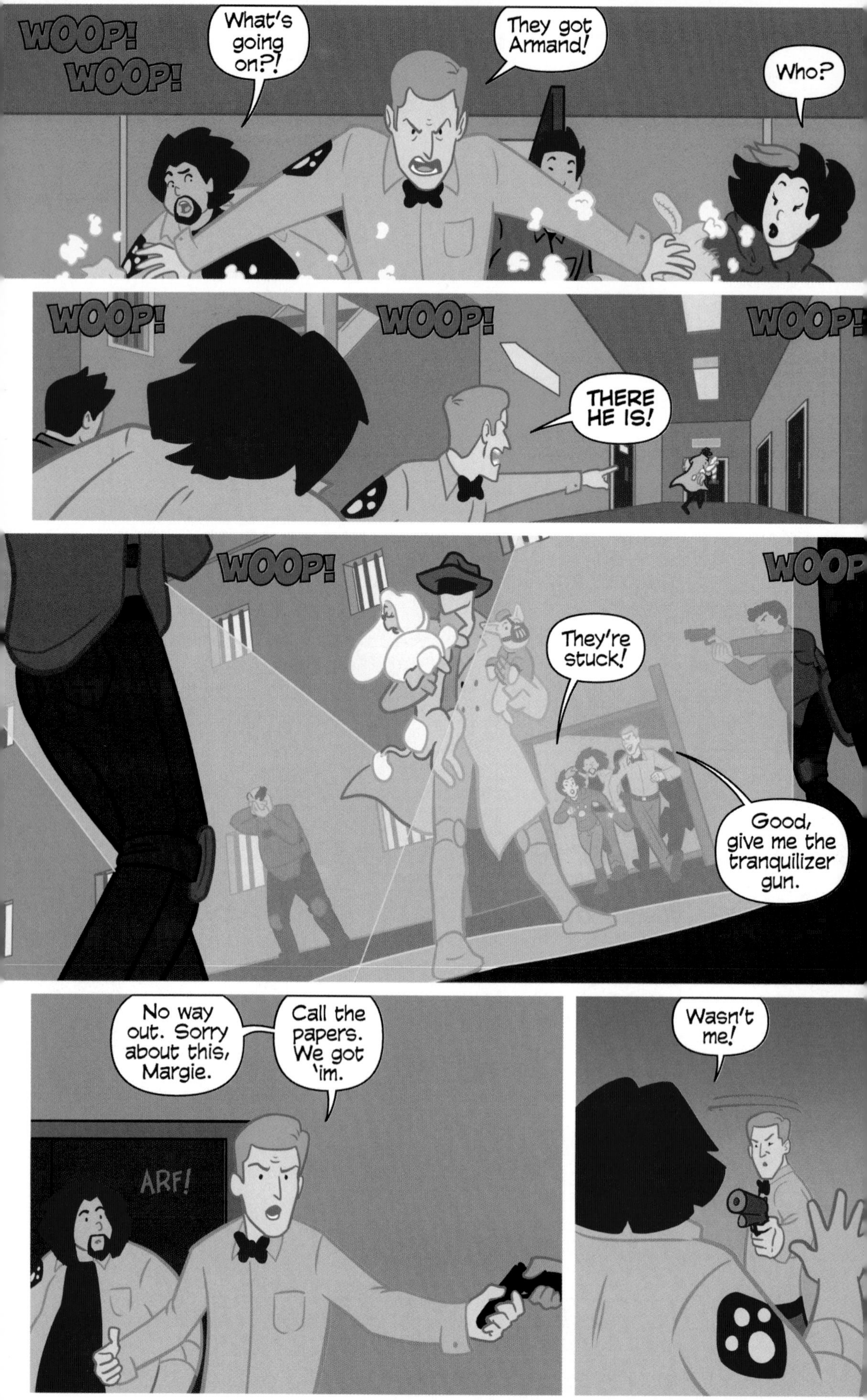
WOOP! WOOP!
What's going on?!
They got Armand!
Who?
WOOP!
WOOP!
WOOP!
THERE HE IS!
WOOP!
WOOP
They're stuck!
Good, give me the tranquilizer gun.
No way out. Sorry about this, Margie.
Call the papers. We got 'im.
ARF!
Wasn't me!

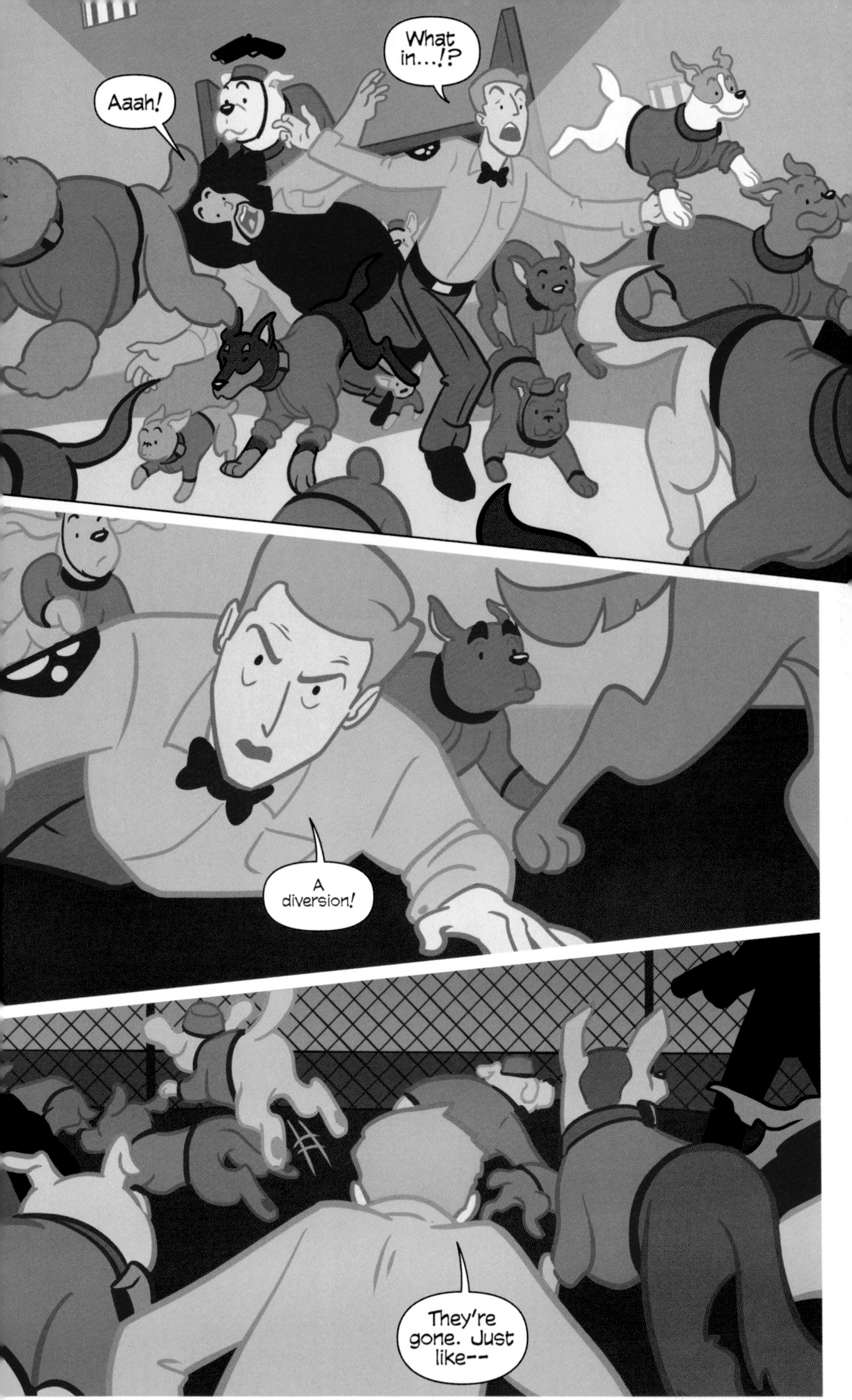
Aaah!
What in...!?
A diversion!
They're gone. Just like--

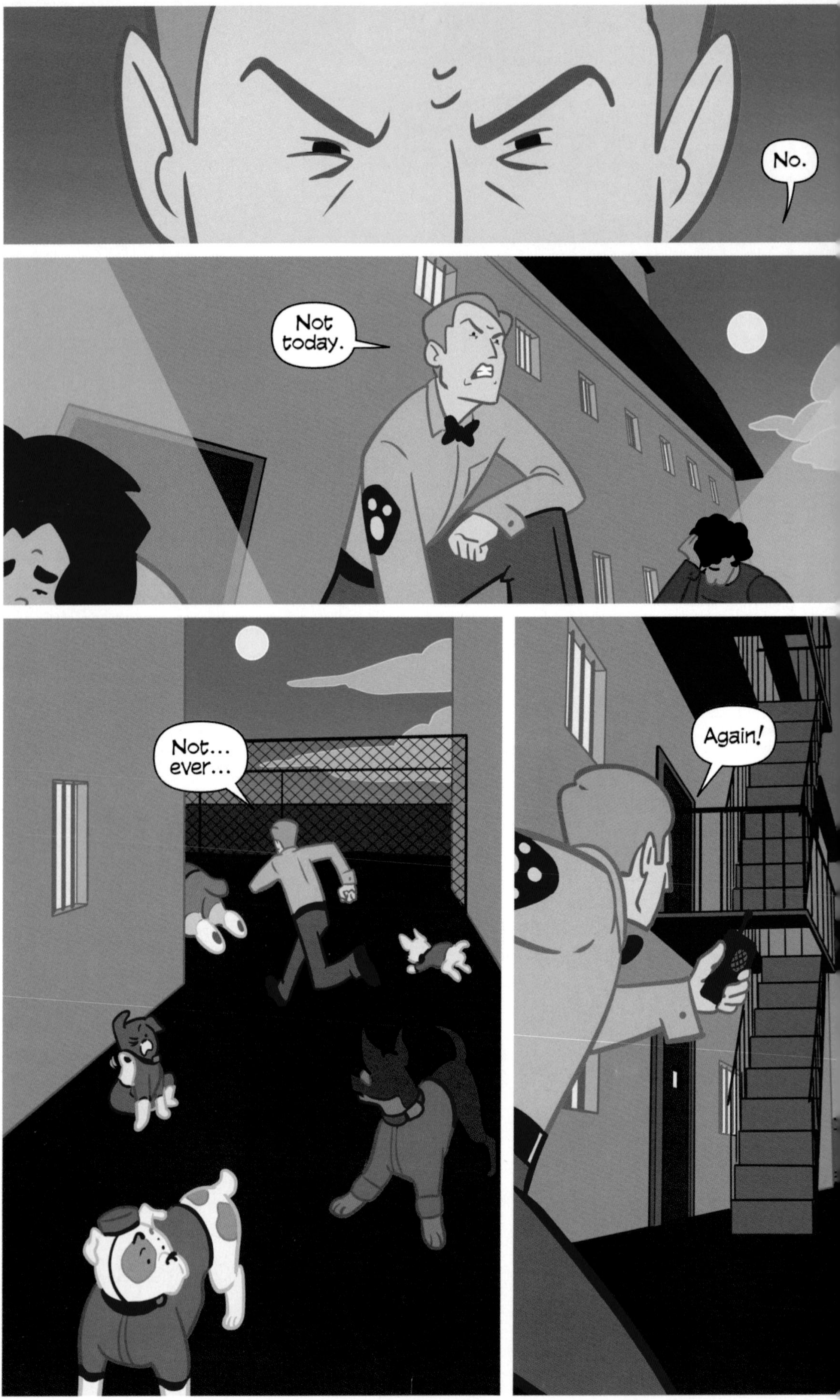
No.
Not today.
Not... ever...
Again!

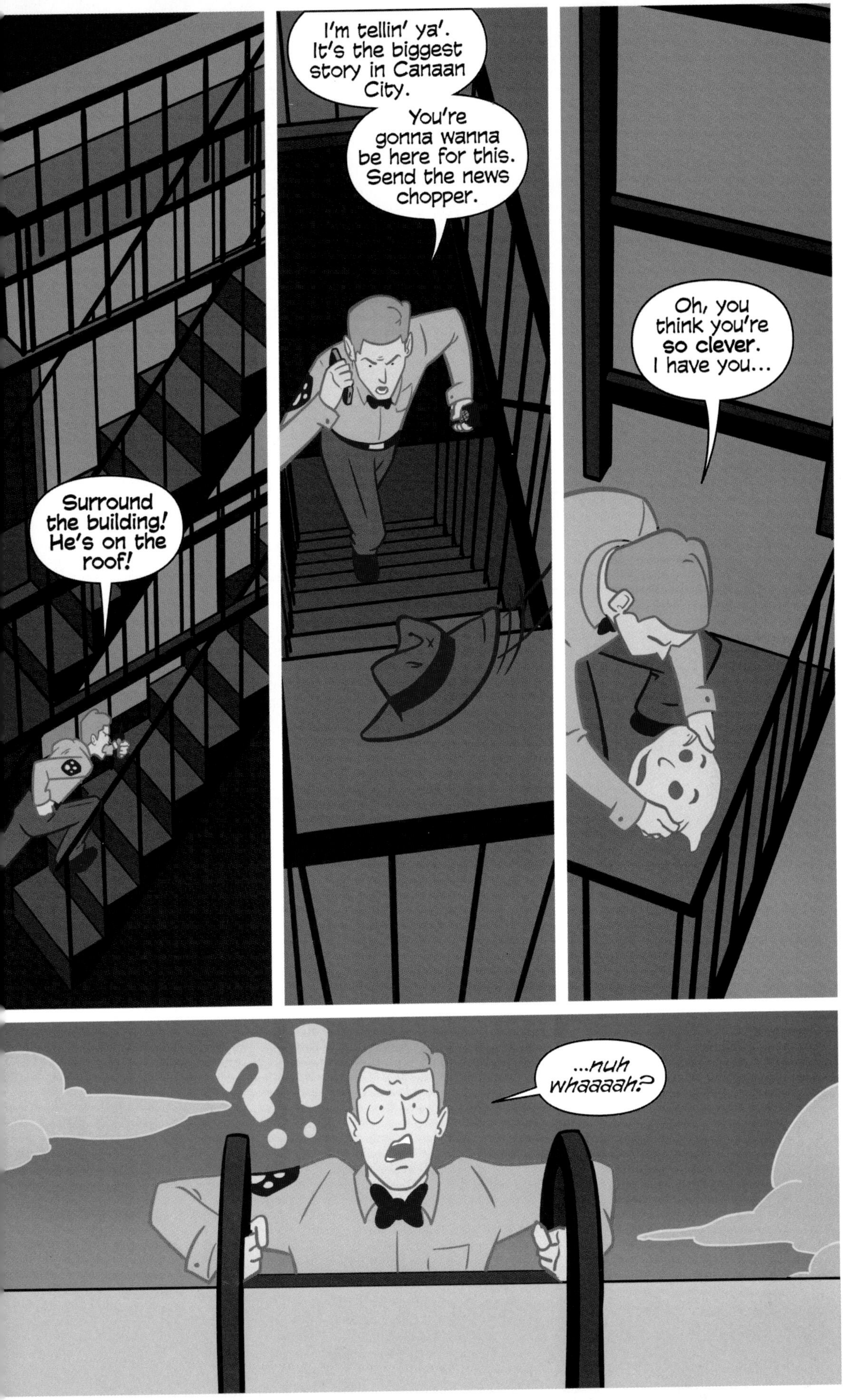
Surround the building! He's on the roof!
I'm tellin' ya'. It's the biggest story in Canaan City.
You're gonna wanna be here for this. Send the news chopper.
Oh, you think you're so **clever**. I have you...
?!
...nuh whaaaah?

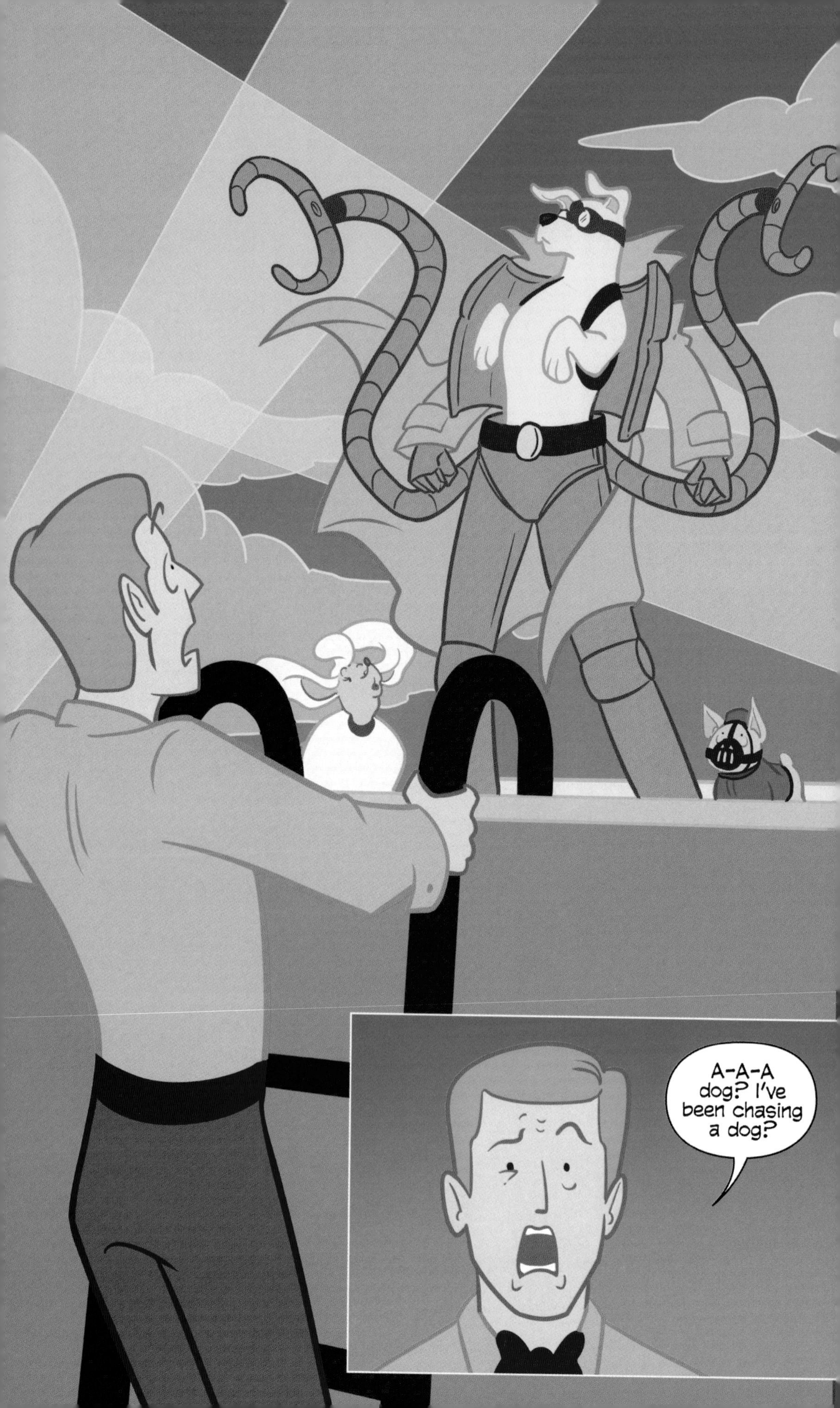
A-A-A dog? I've been chasing a dog?

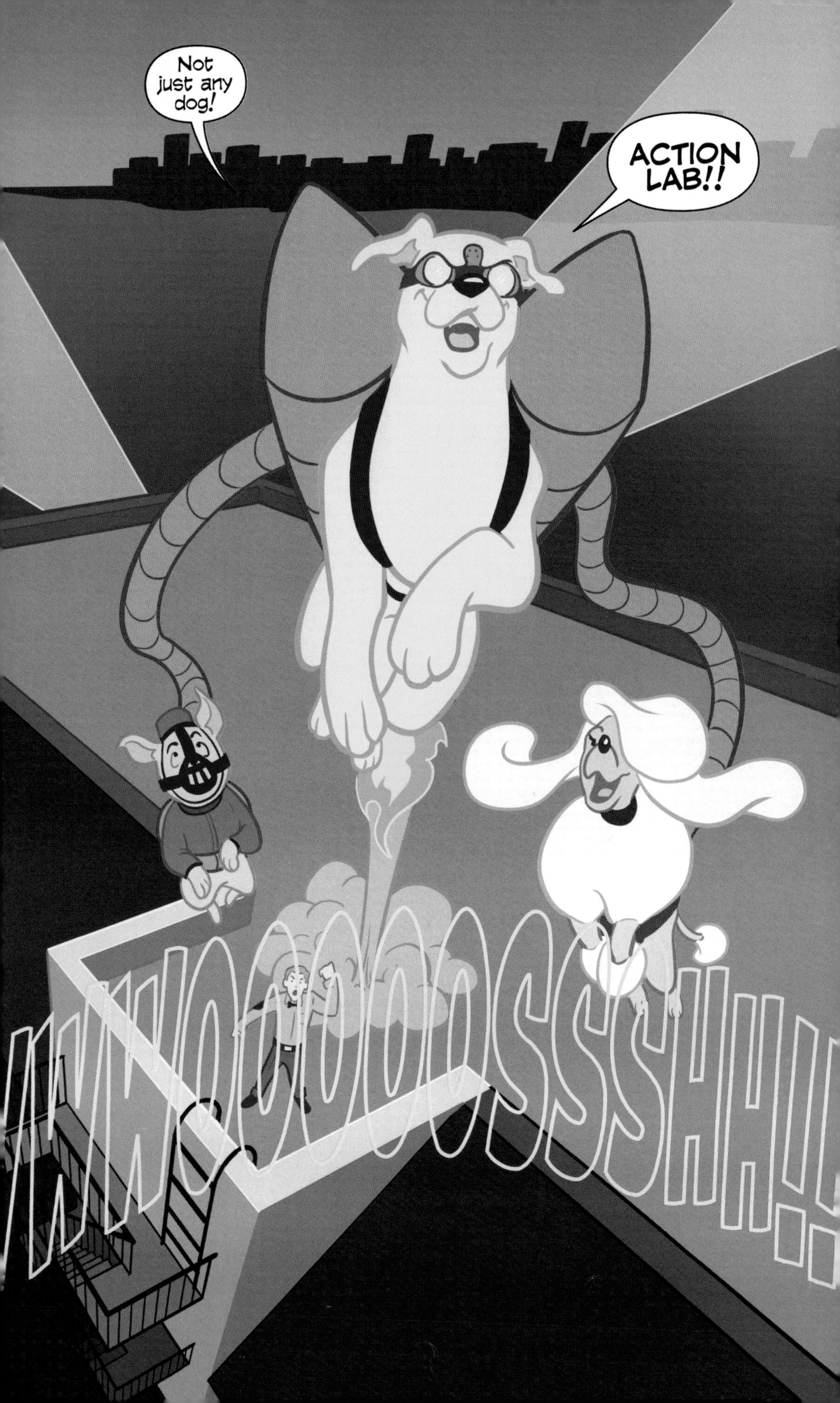
Not just any dog!
ACTION LAB!!
WHOOOOOOSSSSHH!!

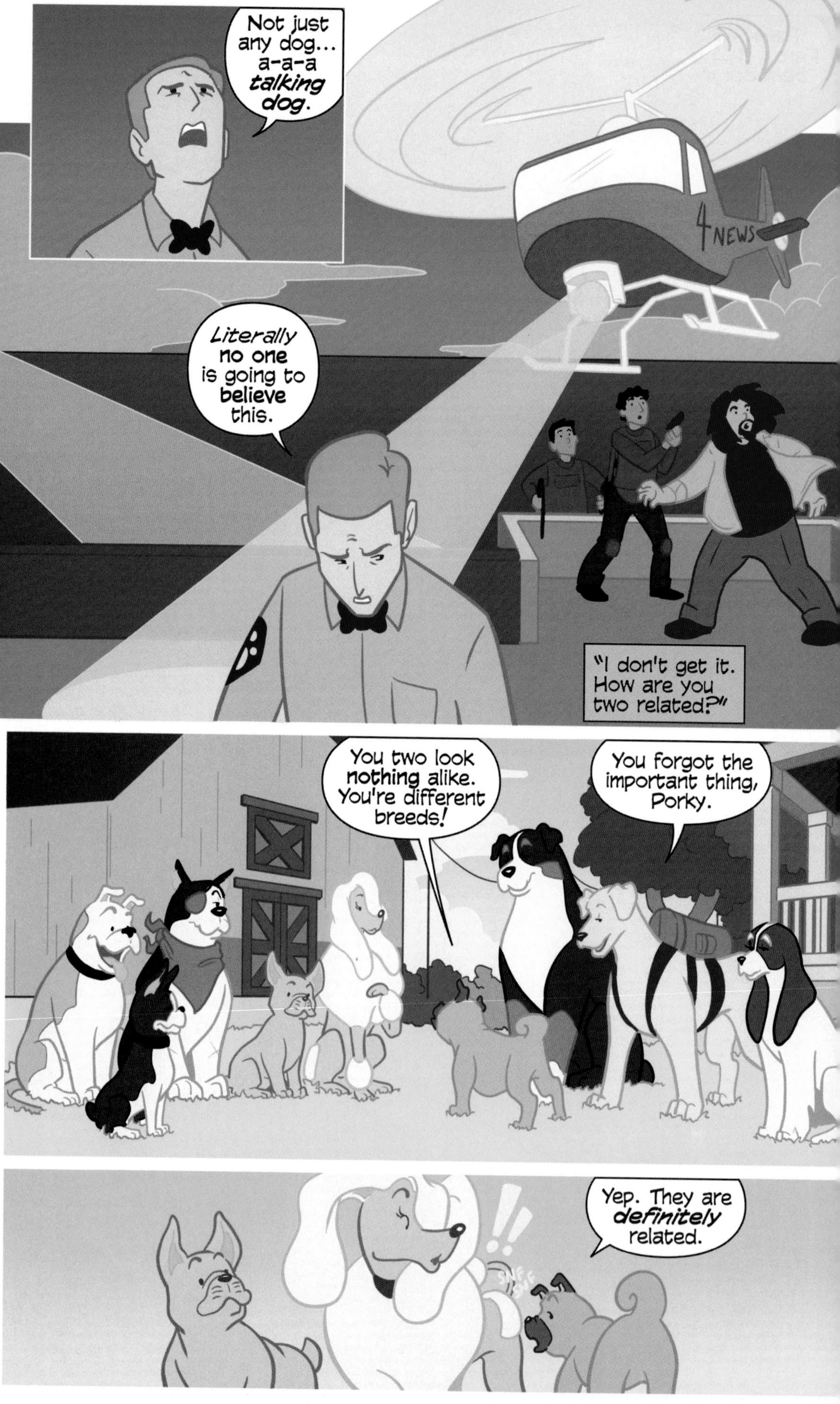
Not just any dog... a-a-a *talking dog*.
Literally **no one** is going to **believe** this.
"I don't get it. How are you two related?"
You two look **nothing** alike. You're different breeds!
You forgot the important thing, Porky.
Yep. They are *definitely* related.

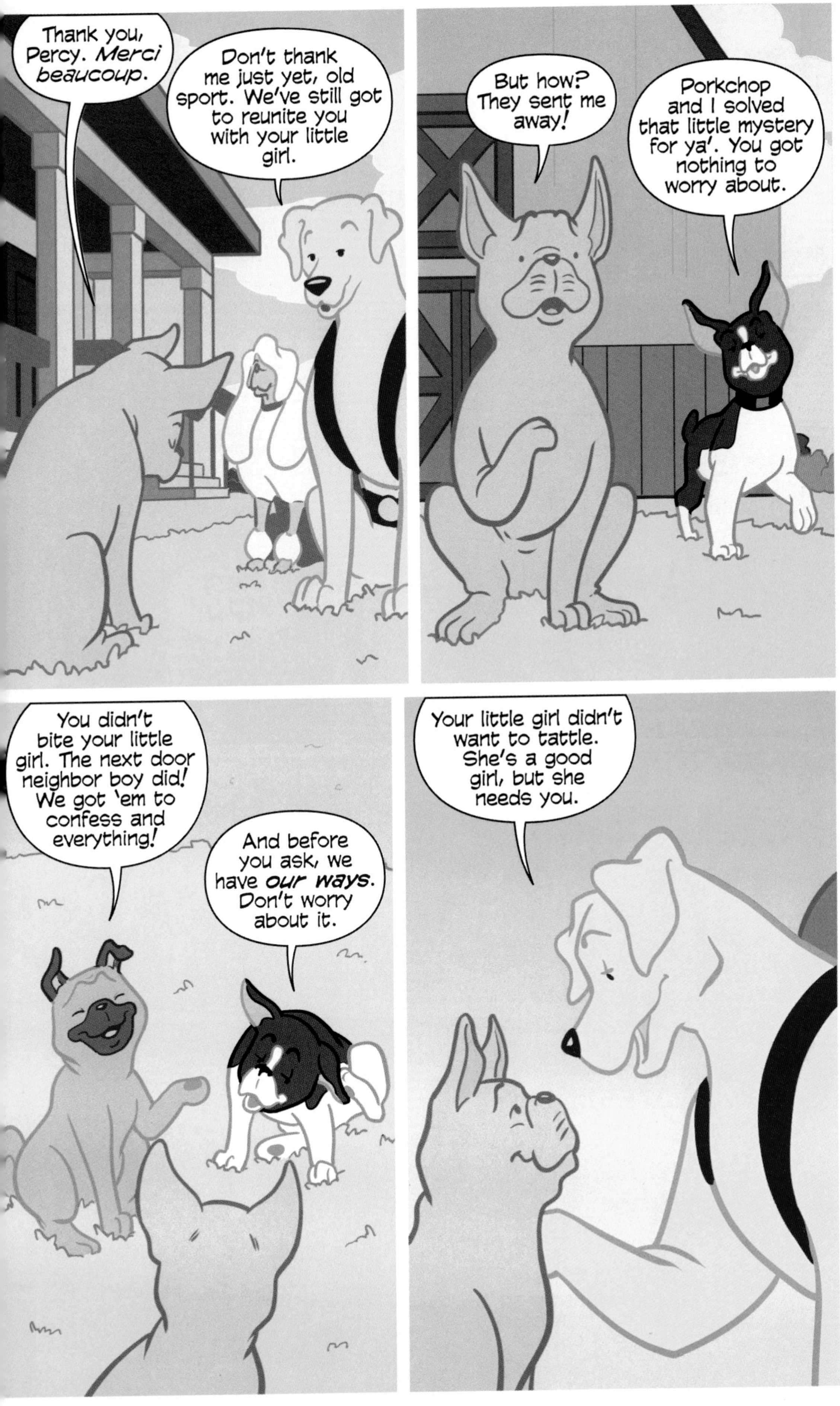
Thank you, Percy. Merci beaucoup.
Don't thank me just yet, old sport. We've still got to reunite you with your little girl.
But how? They sent me away!
Porkchop and I solved that little mystery for ya'. You got nothing to worry about.
You didn't bite your little girl. The next door neighbor boy did! We got 'em to confess and everything!
And before you ask, we have our ways. Don't worry about it.
Your little girl didn't want to tattle. She's a good girl, but she needs you.

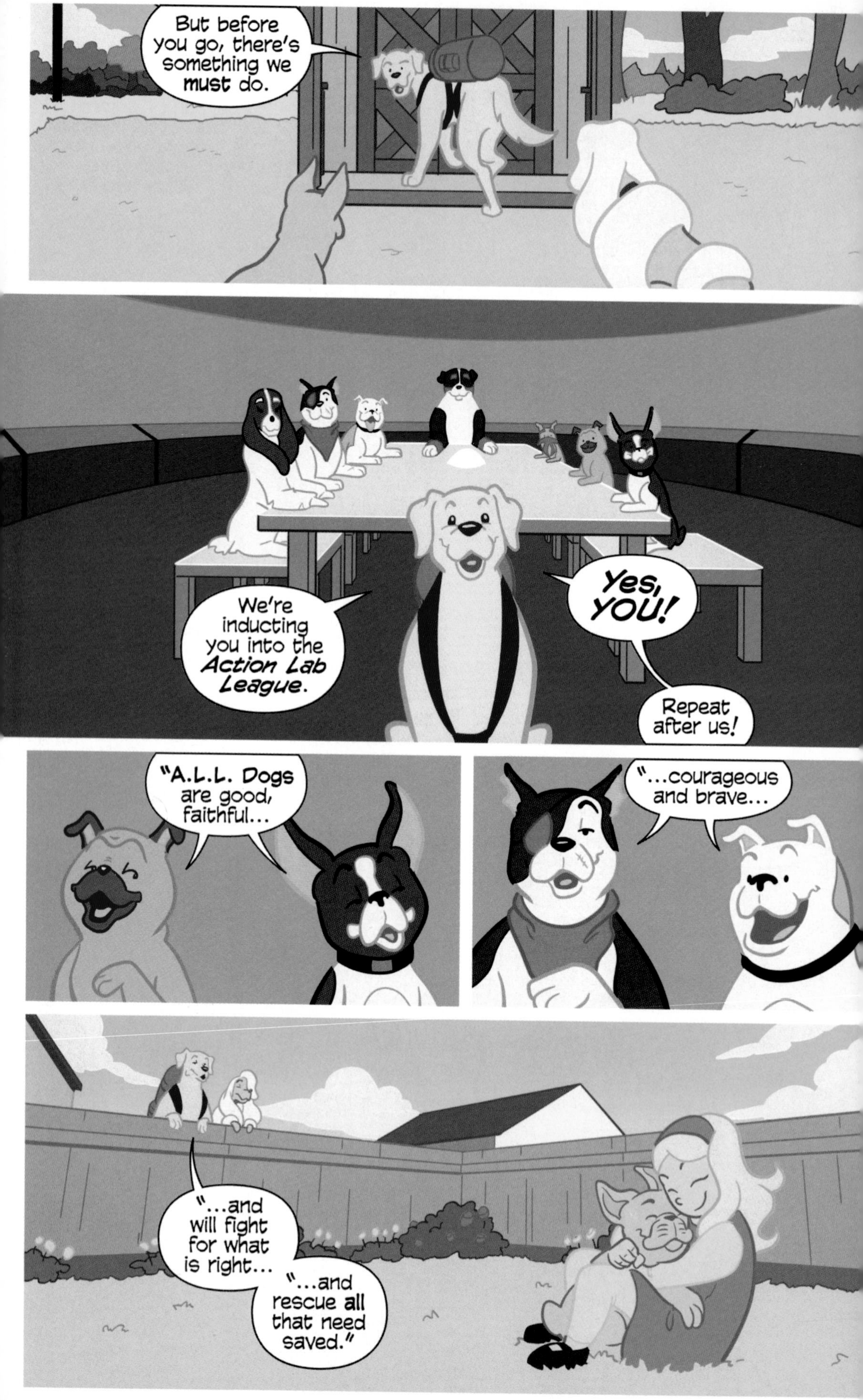
But before you go, there's something we **must** do.
We're inducting you into the ***Action Lab League***.
Yes, YOU!
Repeat after us!
"**A.L.L. Dogs** are good, faithful...
"...courageous and brave...
"...and will fight for what is right...
"...and rescue **all** that need saved."

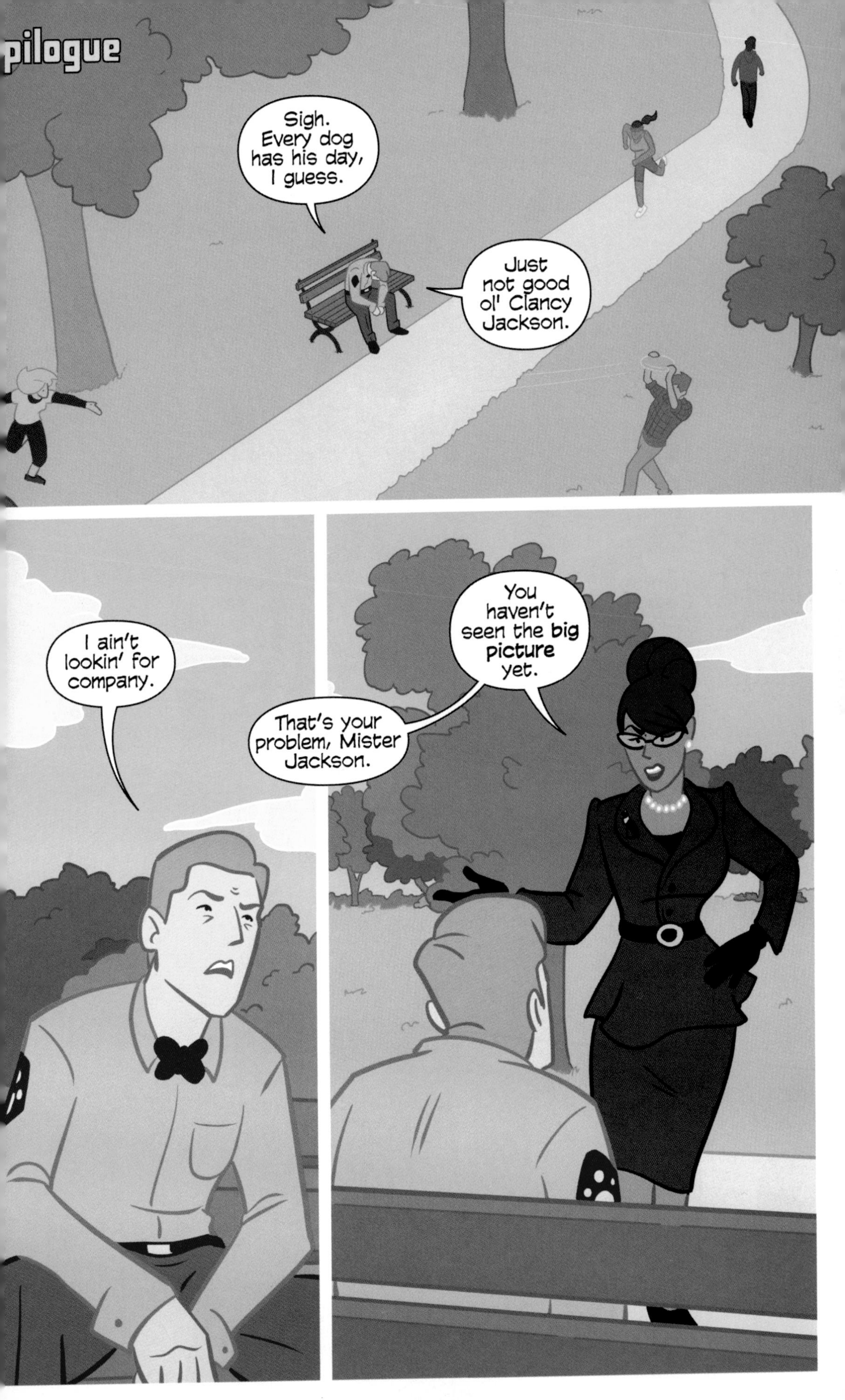
pilogue
Sigh. Every dog has his day, I guess.
Just not good ol' Clancy Jackson.
I ain't lookin' for company.
That's your problem, Mister Jackson.
You haven't seen the big picture yet.

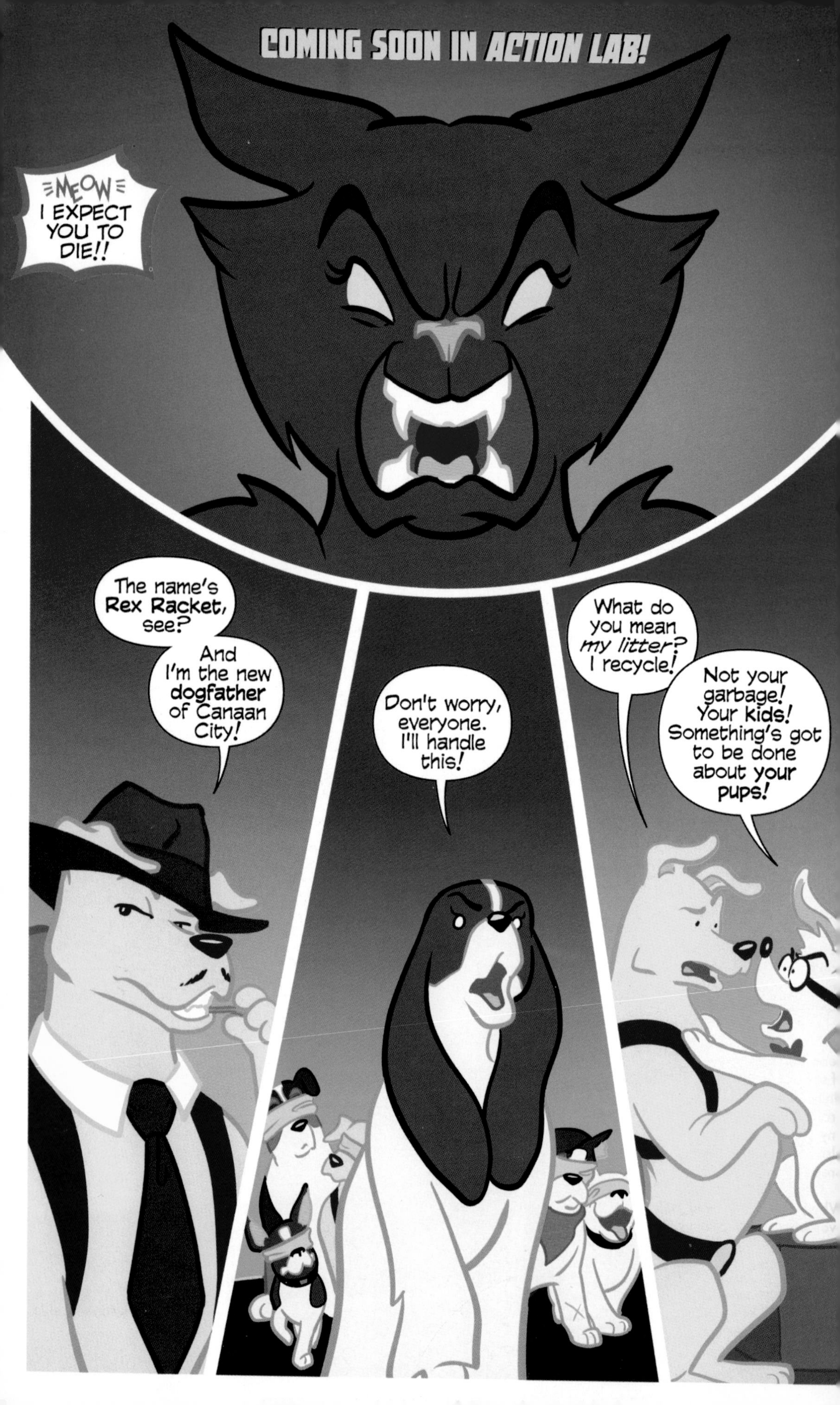

COMING SOON IN ACTION LAB!
MEOW
I EXPECT YOU TO DIE!!
The name's Rex Racket, see?
And I'm the new dogfather of Canaan City!
Don't worry, everyone. I'll handle this!
What do you mean my litter? I recycle!
Not your garbage! Your kids! Something's got to be done about your pups!

In The DOGHOUSE

BY MITZI BOLAÑOS

Greetings from the Doghouse! I write to you from the StubbyDog headquarters, where our volunteers help change the negative stereotypes that surround pit bulls. Here is where you'll find answers to common questions on all things dog! If you have other questions, you can email mitzibolanos@stubbydog.org.

Are pit bulls "different" from other dogs?

All dogs are individuals. Dogs aren't their breed or their past. It's also not "how they're raised." All the victims of dog fighting who have been rescued and are now living peaceful lives with families, including kids and other animals, are proof of that. Those dogs weren't raised to be family dogs, but they were finally given the opportunity to be who they truly are, who they were all along: a family dog.

Dogs are individuals.

Is it true that pit bulls are banned in some places?

Some cities and towns have made it illegal to own pit bulls or dogs that look like pit bulls. The politicians who pass these laws think that these laws will make their communities safer, but experts have research to show that it's not true. Sometimes people fear what they don't know or don't understand. It's important to gather all the facts before passing a law, but sometimes these laws get passed as knee-jerk reactions to a situation.

A dog's physical characteristics, such as the size of his head, does not determine his personality, just as the color of someone's skin or hair does not determine theirs. In the United States, almost half of all the states have laws prohibiting their cities and towns from banning pit bulls or any type or breed of dog. The federal government has also stated that it's wrong to ban pit bulls or any type of breed of dog.

Why is it wrong to ban pit bulls from cities and towns, or even apartment buildings?

Scientists and experts have never been able to show that one type of dog is more dangerous than another type of dog. The American Temperament Test Society gives thousands of dogs a test to see if they're aggressive. The average passing score on this test for all breeds of dogs is an 83%, but pit bull type dogs score above average on this test, at 86%.

If banning pit bulls doesn't make communities safer, what does?

There is scientific research to show that in order to keep communities safe, we should:

*Give dogs positive human attention.
*Never keep a dog on a chain or alone in a yard for extended periods.
*Spay/Neuter dogs.
*Enforce strict laws against animal abuse and neglect.

Experts such as veterinarians, animal control agents, and lawyers agree that this is the best way to keep communities safe and that banning pit bulls or any other type of dog is ineffective and makes criminals want those dogs for bad purposes.

Why do we keep talking about pit bulls?

Often times, these are dogs who have seen the worst of human nature and have no reason to trust us. And yet, not only do they still want to be with us, they even want to heal us. So many abused pit bulls have become therapy dogs who visit nursing homes and hospitals, and even help kids in library reading programs.

These dogs break down stereotypes and misconceptions like gentle giants – not with force, but with love, patience, and trust.

So if you haven't spent any time with a pit bull type dog, go meet one. You'll see he's not so scary. He'll want to lick your face, and he probably wants his butt scratched. Because he's just a dog. He doesn't understand why people fear him. And neither will you.

StubbyDog™
Rediscover the pit bull.

For more information, visit StubbyDog.org!

Thanks, Mitzi! Hey everyone! Scott here! In the last issue, you got to meet Vito's precious puppies. So now it's time to meet mine! First up, Gwen Dogg.

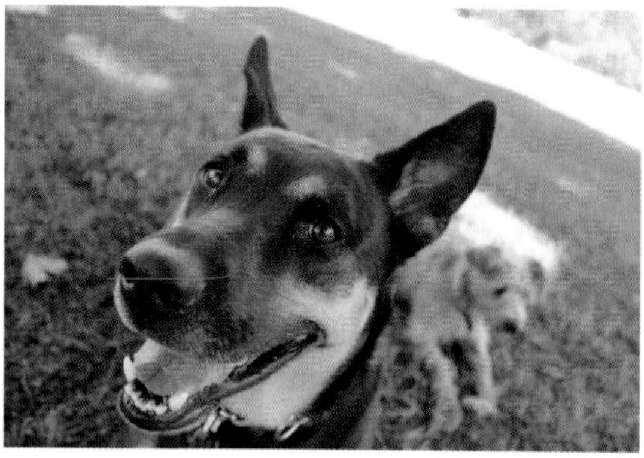

A long, long time ago, a friend of mine named Morgann posted on MySpace that her dog had just had a litter of puppies and that they needed to find a good home for all these little puppies. My wife, Kelly, and I saw one particular picture and said, "Oh, she needs to join our family!" As soon as she was old enough, we drove her home and named her Gwen. We're not sure what kind of dog Gwen is. Most people think she looks like a German shepherd, but her chest is real thick, which makes us think she has a little Rottweiler in her. All we know is that we couldn't ask for a kinder dog. She loves to play with us, wrestle with us, and when we brought our daughter, Amelia home, Gwen became her mama. Gwen doesn't like strangers getting near Amelia (she'll even get upset with us if we start playing too rough with her!). We love Gwen very much. She's a good dog.

Our other dog is Richard Alpe Tumnus, but we call him Tumnus fo short (all of our pets are named afte characters in books and movies – if yo can guess who our dogs are name after, you can get one of our covete Nose Prizes!). Tumnus is a terrier tha we adopted from a shelter. He ha been found on the side of the roa before being taken to the shelter. H was a little skittish around us at firs and he's still scared of most olde women, but with a little love and a lot c patience, he's become a little cuddl puppy. He has a lot of energy and wi run circles around Gwen. The onl problem with Tumnus is he doesn always respect or understand persona boundaries.

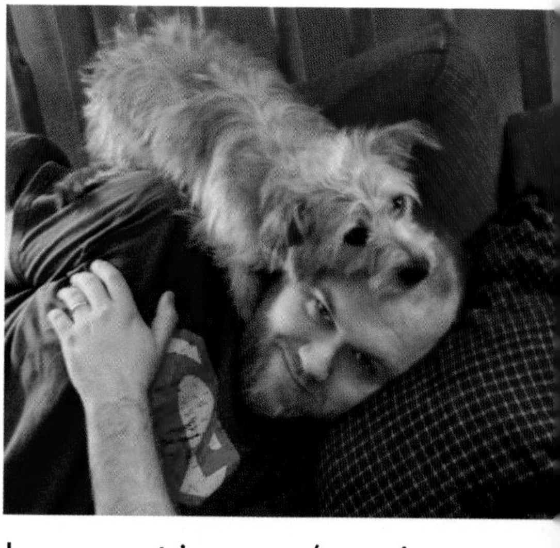

In our next issue, we're going to mee some of YOUR pets! We're reall excited! If you want to send us pics an tell us why your dog is an "action lab," you can do so at the email addres below! (Ask your parents for help!)

-Scot

NEXT ISSUE: Percy and the League meet a new dog friend...or is she a foe? Speaking of foes, Clancy has a brand new ally in his fight against Action Lab. It's not looking good for our hero! See you in 60!

Email us at PercyTheDogOfWonder@gmail.com!

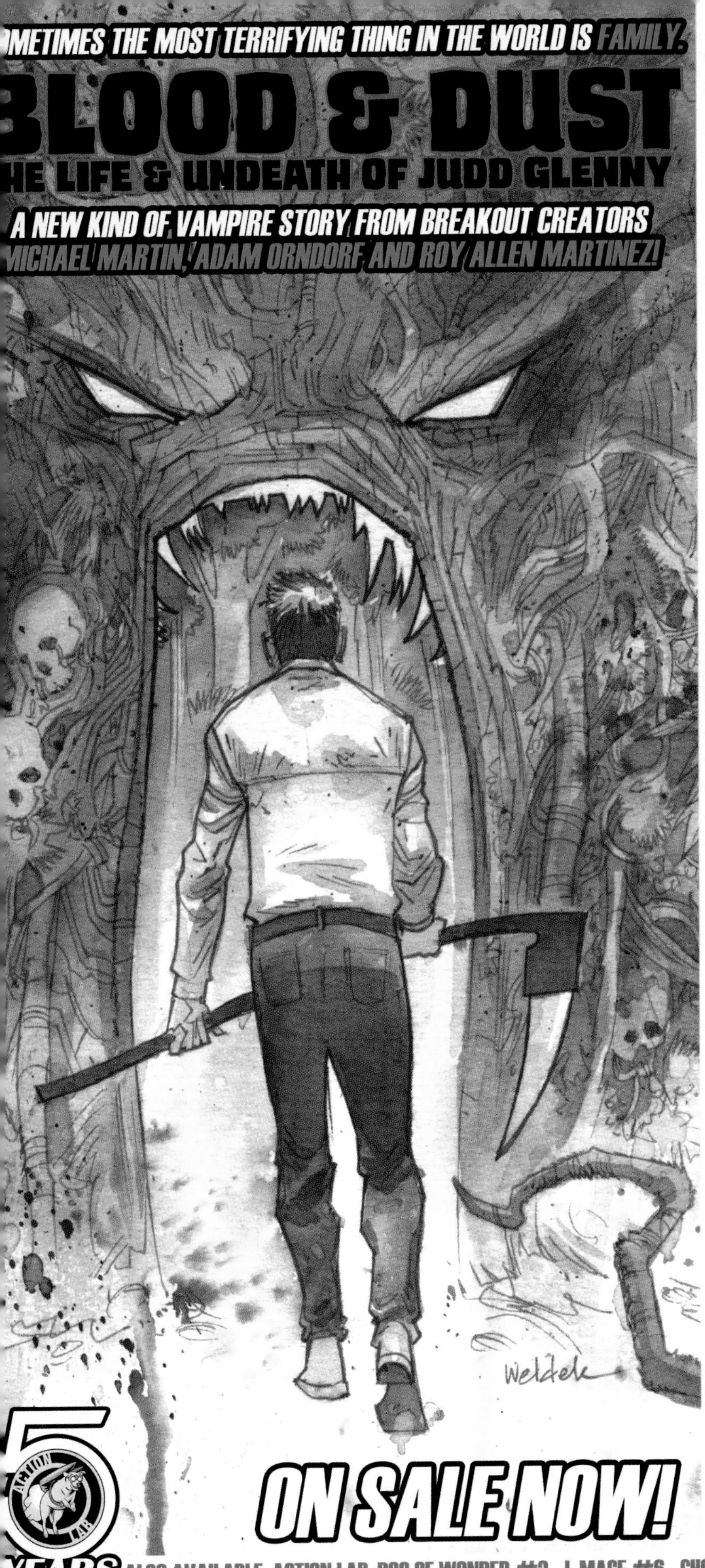

OMETIMES THE MOST TERRIFYING THING IN THE WORLD IS FAMILY.
BLOOD & DUST
HE LIFE & UNDEATH OF JUDD GLENNY
A NEW KIND OF VAMPIRE STORY FROM BREAKOUT CREATORS
MICHAEL MARTIN, ADAM ORNDORF AND ROY ALLEN MARTINEZ!
5 YEARS
ON SALE NOW!

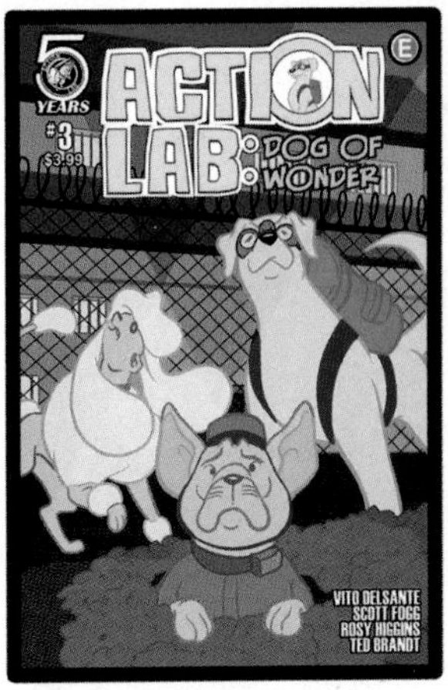

5 YEARS
ACTION LAB: DOG OF WONDER
#3
$3.99
VITO DELSANTE
SCOTT FOGG
ROSY HIGGINS
TED BRANDT

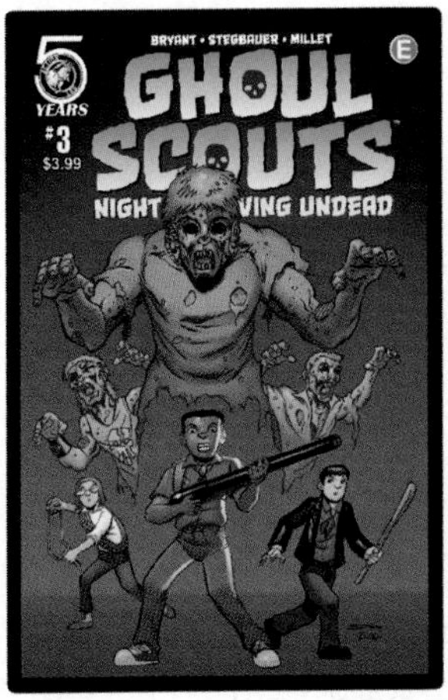

BRYANT • STEGBAUER • MILLET
5 YEARS
#3
$3.99
GHOUL SCOUTS
NIGHT VING UNDEAD

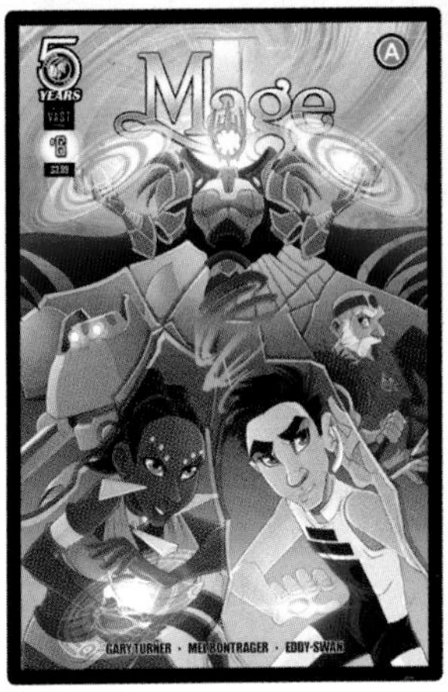

5 YEARS
Mage
GARY TURNER • MEL BONTRAGER • EDDY SWAN

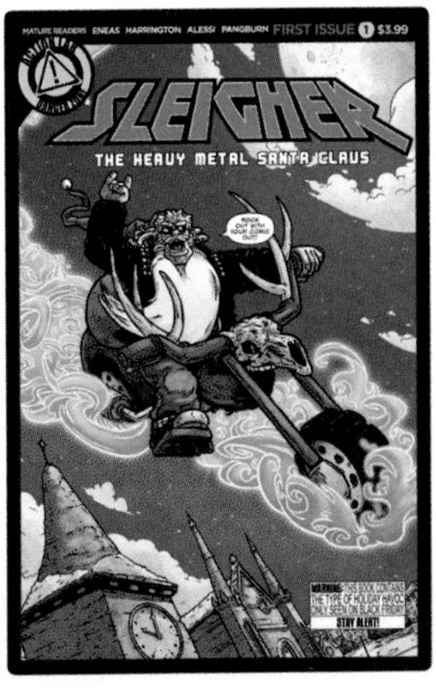

MATURE READERS ENEAS HARRINGTON ALESSI PANGBURN FIRST ISSUE 1 $3.99
SLEIGHER
THE HEAVY METAL SANTA CLAUS
STAY ALERT!

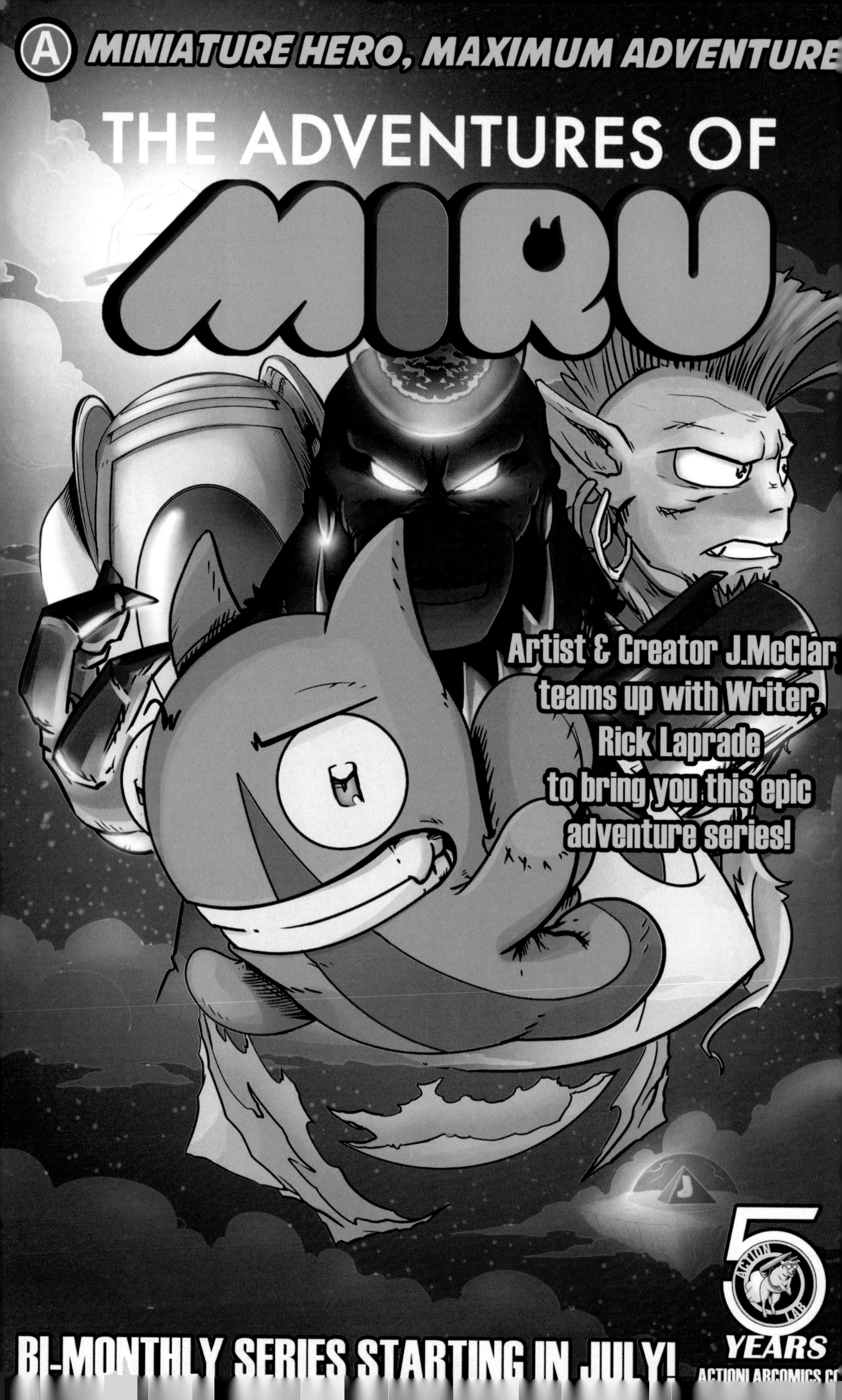
A
MINIATURE HERO, MAXIMUM ADVENTURE
THE ADVENTURES OF
MIRU
Artist & Creator J.McClar
teams up with Writer,
Rick Laprade
to bring you this epic
adventure series!
BI-MONTHLY SERIES STARTING IN JULY!
5
ACTION LAB
YEARS
ACTIONLABCOMICS.CO

MONTY
The Dinosaur

Action Lab's newest all ages adventure
100 million years in the making.

Making new friends starting in August 2016

Ask your local comic shop to order a copy,
or look for Monty The Dinosaur in Previews Magazine!

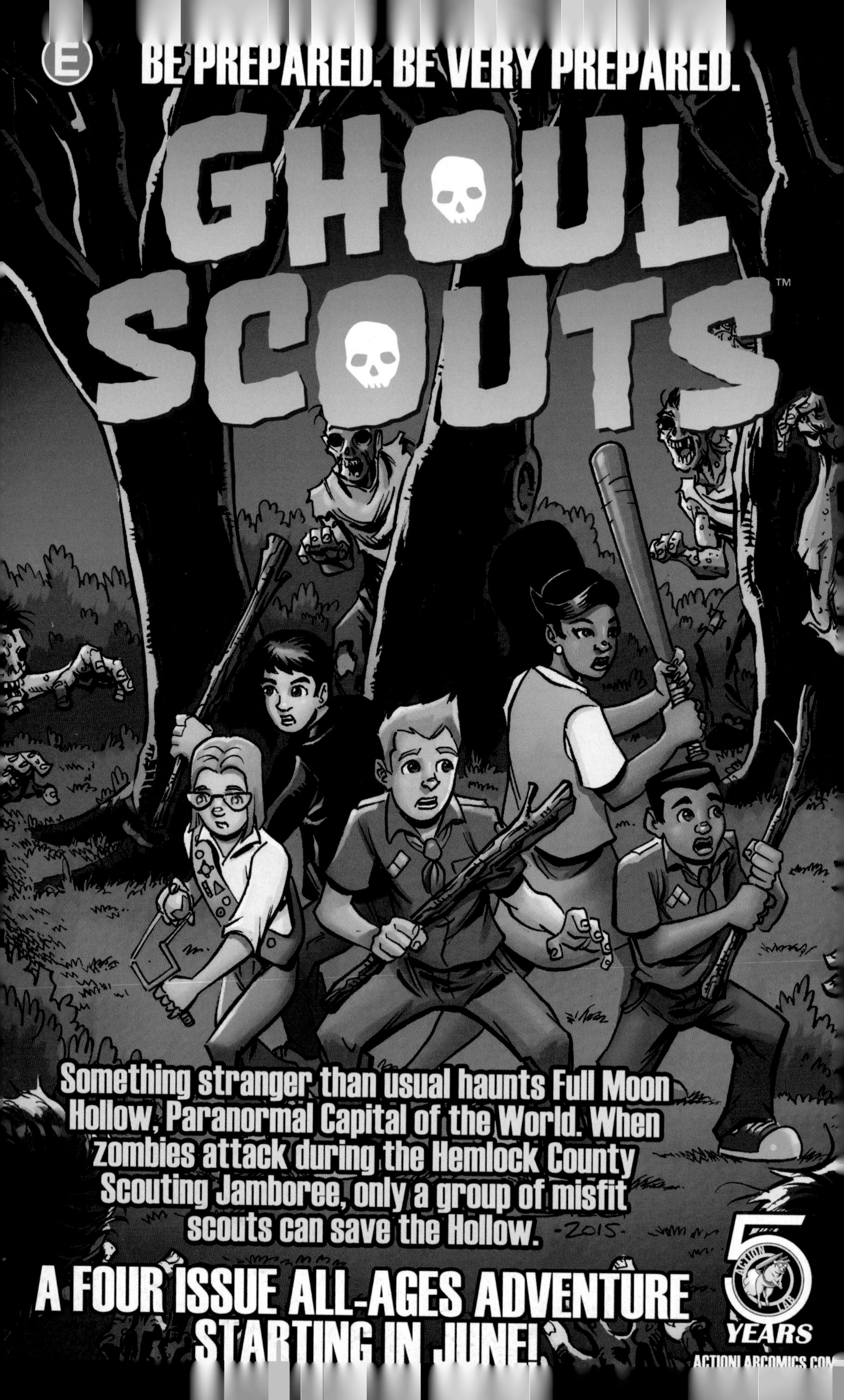
E
BE PREPARED. BE VERY PREPARED.
GHOUL SCOUTS™
Something stranger than usual haunts Full Moon Hollow, Paranormal Capital of the World. When zombies attack during the Hemlock County Scouting Jamboree, only a group of misfit scouts can save the Hollow.
-2015-
A FOUR ISSUE ALL-AGES ADVENTURE STARTING IN JUNE!
5 YEARS
ACTION LAB
ACTIONLABCOMICS.COM

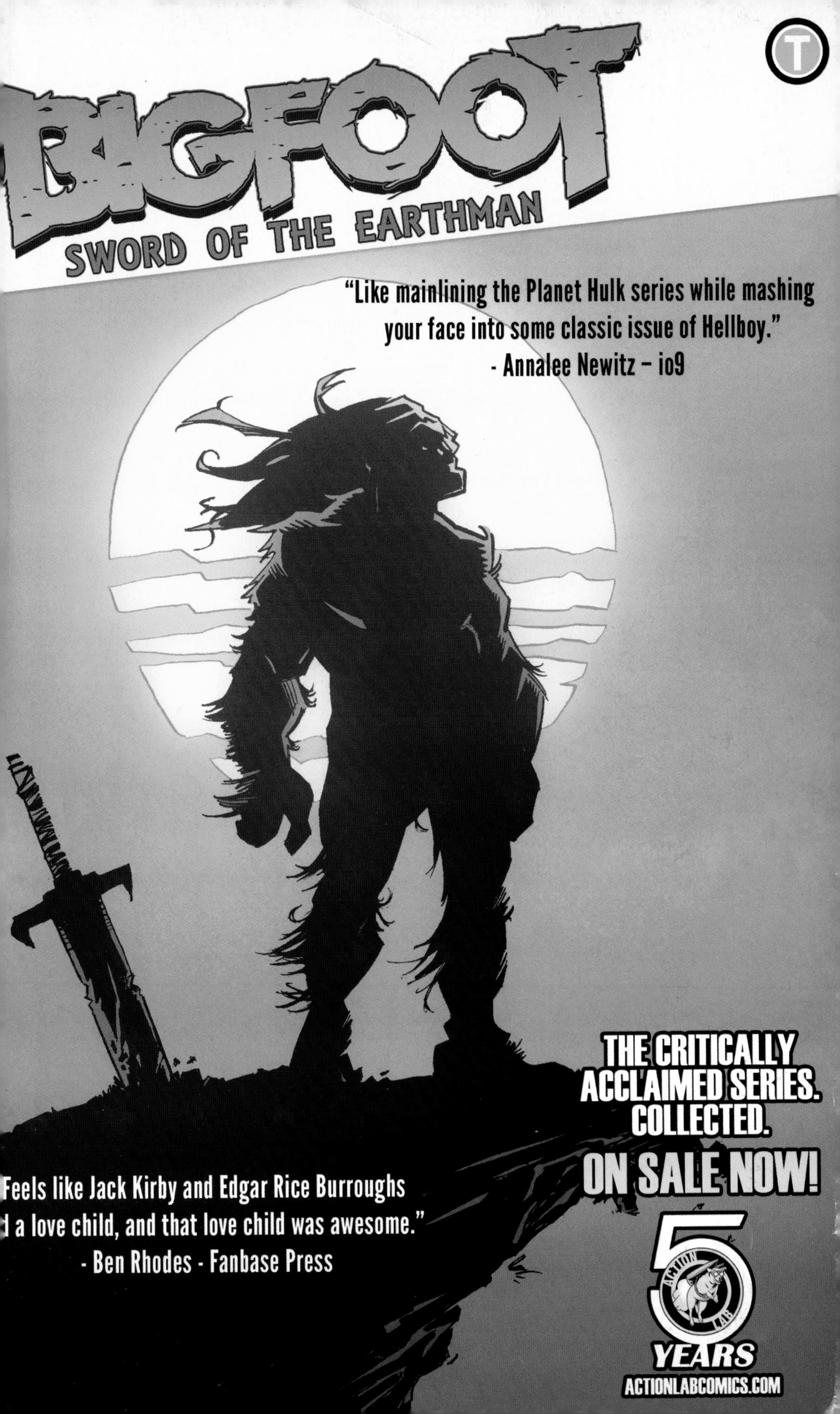
T
BIGFOOT
SWORD OF THE EARTHMAN
"Like mainlining the Planet Hulk series while mashing your face into some classic issue of Hellboy."
- Annalee Newitz – io9
THE CRITICALLY ACCLAIMED SERIES. COLLECTED.
ON SALE NOW!
Feels like Jack Kirby and Edgar Rice Burroughs
a love child, and that love child was awesome."
- Ben Rhodes - Fanbase Press
5 YEARS
ACTION LAB
ACTIONLABCOMICS.COM